F͏͏c ...19

with all our love

Bary + Joyce

Praise for *To Really Love a Woman:*

"Read this book if you want to have a more loving, intimate, understanding and vulnerable relationship with the special person in your life." –John Gray, PhD, author of *Men are from Mars, Women are from Venus.*

"To say that Barry and Joyce Vissell are masters of love is not an exaggeration. Not only is their own marriage a model of the kind of relationship most of us would like to have, but they teach us what real, lasting love is all about. I highly recommend these two new books, and all their books and retreats to anyone who wants to have an enlightened relationship that lasts through time." –Jed Diamond, PhD, author of *The Enlightened Marriage: The 5 Transformative Stages of Relationships and Why the Best is Still to Come*

"Barry and Joyce Vissell are two of the most sincere and compelling voices for healing relationships and creating the highest connections. They have devoted their lives to understanding and explaining what makes relationships work. The wisdom they share in these new books will absolutely help you create the kind of relationships your heart desires and you deserve." –Alan Cohen, author of *Don't Get Lucky, Get Smart*

"*To Really Love a Woman* and *To Really Love a Man* are backed by the powerful work the Vissells have been doing decade after decade in helping couples thrive and see the highest in one another, fueled by the beauty and success of their own partnership." –David Feinstein and Donna Eden, authors of *The Energies of Love*

"Joyce and Barry Vissell walk their talk. Having been together for 52 years and taught thousands of people how to love themselves and their partners, I am thrilled that they have shared their wisdom in these books. Their writing is a true representation of who they are: warm, caring, supportive, funny, and inspiring. Give yourself the gift of these books and watch all of your relationships transform!" –Karen Drucker, singer, songwriter, and author of *"Let Go of the Shore"*

"It's so easy to fall into tried-and-true patterns of showing love. The Vissells challenge us to let our imagination be big and to reach down deep to expand our repertoire of ways we show love. It's a detailed, practical, and inspirational guide for those who aspire to become great lovers and to bring maximum delight to their partnership." –Linda Bloom, co-author of *Secrets of Great Marriages*.

"Reading these two books is a blessing and transmission of decades of personal and couples work. These books are filled with teachings. Joyce and Barry have put truths into words that we were unable to articulate. We want to thank them from our hearts for creating an authentic map that we can trust and feel confident to follow." –Barbara and Mark Stefik, authors of *The Zorcon World Stories*

To Really Love a Woman

by Joyce Vissell, RN,MS & Barry Vissell, MD

authors of The Shared Heart, Models of Love,
Risk To Be Healed, The Heart's Wisdom, Meant
To Be, and A Mother's Final Gift

To Really Love a Woman

Copyright © 2017 by Ramira Publishing
PO Box 2140, Aptos, CA 95001-2140. 831.684.2299.
www.SharedHeart.org.

ISBN-13: 978-0-9612720-7-4
Library of Congress Control Number: 2017942521

Printed in the United States of America on acid-free, chlorine-free, and Sustainable Forestry Initiative (SFI) certified paper.

Cover design by Melinda Lawton.
Back cover photo by Barry Vissell.

Also by Barry and Joyce Vissell:

The Shared Heart: Relationship Initiations and Celebrations
Models of Love: The Parent-Child Journey
Risk to be Healed: The Heart of Personal and Relationship Growth
Light in the Mirror: A New Way to Understand Relationships
Meant To Be: Miraculous True Stories to Inspire a Lifetime of Love
A Mother's Final Gift: How One Woman's Courageous Dying Transformed her Family
And by Rami Vissell:
Rami's Book: The Inner Life of a Child

Acknowledgements

We are grateful to our editing angels, John Drew, Nancy Collins, Elisabeth Hallett, Meg Rinaldi, Jackson Roesch, Lisa Kingsbury, Liliana Cartagena, Pam Schott, and Dawn Song.

Thank you Melinda Lawton for the beautiful book cover.

Thanks to all the couples who contributed their words of wisdom, and to the couples who became examples in these pages.

And always our thanks to the One who continually teaches us to really love.

For our parents:

Louise and Hank Wollenberg and
Helen and Michael Vissell
Always loving us from beyond

our children:

Rami, Mira, and John-Nuriel
How proud we are of all three of you

and our grandchildren:

Skye and Owen
Keeping our hearts wide open

To Really Love a Woman

Contents

"... When you find yourself lying helpless in her arms,
... When you can see her unborn children in her eyes,
You know you really love a woman."

– Bryan Adams

Introduction

HOW DOES A WOMAN REALLY NEED TO BE LOVED? How can her partner help to bring out her deepest passion, her sensuality, her creativity, her dreams, her joy, and at the same time allow her to feel safe, accepted and appreciated?

We feel that women and men are essentially similar souls in different-sexed bodies. Both sexes want the same happiness, need the same love, crave the same peace, and feel the same emotions. In all our previous books we have emphasized the similarity rather than the difference between the sexes. While this is the highest truth, there is another truth no less important. Most men and women approach life and relationship in different ways and react to situations differently. Notice we said "most," because nothing is all or none. However, the difference in male and female hormones, the findings of brain chemistry research, added to the difference in how women and men are raised, help create different emotional climates and even alter ways of thinking. On the deepest level, women and men are alike. In personality, there is often a clear contrast. On the level of soul there is sameness. In thoughts and feelings, men and women can be strikingly different.

We write these books not to point out the differences between the sexes. There are enough books doing that. We write these books to give tools to the readers to more deeply honor their partners. With honoring there can be joining. Respect for differences breaks down the age-old wall between women and men. Before there can be union, there must be love. Before there can be love, there must be understanding and respect. Before there can be understanding and respect, there must be listening -- real listening – both inner and outer.

To really love another is to more deeply love yourself. To more deeply understand another is to more deeply understand your own soul. In other words, the real opportunity of relationship is your own spiritual growth. As souls, we are both male and female. It is just in our bodies, minds, and emotions that we express one sex predominantly.

Although these writings refer mostly to heterosexual women and men, there is a wealth of information for LGBTQ. Our focus, after all, is how to deeply love another person, whether it be a man or a woman.

The Platinum Rule of Relationship

There's a new rule that's specific for intimate relationships. Most of us know the Golden Rule: Do unto others as you would have them do unto you. It works fine in many circumstances. If you're tempted to yell at the guy who just cut you off in traffic, you take a deep breath and give him the benefit of the doubt. After all, that could be you someday. You follow the Golden Rule when you visit a friend who's sick, because you would want the same treatment if you become sick.

The problem is, however, that the Golden Rule often does not work with intimate relationships, especially when it gets down to specific actions. For example, you may be content with the needle on the gas gauge hovering just above empty. If you run out of gas, it'll just be an annoying inconvenience. Your female partner, however, may be terrified at the proposition of running out of gas. It may bring up images of being stranded on the side of a road, and vulnerable to anyone with less than honorable motives.

Then there's the guy who goes to Home Depot to shop for a wedding anniversary present. If he could choose a gift for his wife to get him, it would be a new cordless drill and driver. So that's what he decides to get his wife. When she opens the gift on their anniversary, he's stymied by her lack of enthusiasm. He is, after all, following the Golden Rule.

There's a better rule for romantic relationships that bumps consciousness up to a higher level – The Platinum Rule – Do unto others as *they* would have you do unto *them*.

In other words, treat others the way they want to be treated, rather than the way you want to be treated. It means you actually have to find out what she wants.

The Platinum Rule can be hard to follow. I have to get personal here. I love touch. Any touch is wonderful to me. I love it when Joyce takes my hand. I love it when she hugs me or even when she jumps on top of me when we're lying together. Now Joyce loves touch as well, but she also loves spoken words. They can be words of love or appreciation. They can be questions inviting her to share what she feels.

It's easy for me to slip into the Golden Rule with regards to touch and words. I can forget about her love of words and, instead, touch her because that's what I love. And don't get me wrong ... she appreciates this show of love through touch, even if it's not the only thing she wants. It's just that I need to remember the Platinum Rule, and switch to give Joyce both the touch and the words she wants. Then I am really loving Joyce.

Is something wrong because you may have to ask her what she really wants, likes, or needs? Does that mean you're not the divine lover you want to be? It's lovely to try to guess these things and sometimes, by trial and error, you'll actually get it right. But we can't be mind readers all the time. If you want to be a divine lover, ask her often about her preferences. Remember, her preferences can change over time. Ask about mundane things, like food, clothing, types of exercise, books, anything. Also ask about important things, like what specific spiritual practice would allow her to feel closer to you.

4   VISSELL

It's even good to gently remind her about what you really need and want. This is very different from complaining or criticizing her. That's a turn-off for anyone. Instead, try inviting her to love you in a different way. Let's revisit Joyce's and my touch/talk preferences, but much more personally. During lovemaking, I may get a little too absorbed in the sensory experience and become quiet. Joyce has a sweet way of saying, "Barry, I would love to hear your words right now." I hear this as an invitation to love her even more, rather than a put-down, or that I'm doing something wrong. My then opening to a flow of poetry, or even singing a love song to her, enhances not only her experience, but mine as well.

Want to be a better lover? Follow the Platinum Rule of relationship.

By the way, they do sell flowers at Home Depot.

To Really Make Love to a Woman

🏃

BARRY AND I HAVE SEEN THAT MOST WOMEN NEED TO BE INVITED INTO THE SEXUAL EXPERIENCE IN A VULNERABLE AND ROMANTIC WAY. It doesn't work to be fit into the day like just another appointment: "Hey honey, I see you've been working hard all day. Why don't we have sex before I rush off to play tennis with the guys." That kind of an invitation is about as inviting to a woman as, "Do you want to go on a date with me to the laundromat?"

It's the same for the man who's on the phone all evening making business calls, and then at 9pm, one hour before he likes to go to sleep, he comes into the living room and invites his partner to have sex, even in a loving way. Chances are his wife or partner will look at him and say, "You've got to be kidding!" Rather than those business calls, a close time talking and connecting is much more inviting and appealing to most women.

Sex is so much more than physical pleasure. A woman wants to feel loved, cherished, understood and special to the man she loves. It is romantic and appealing to be invited into the experience through loving attention and connection.

A Woman's Sexual Stages

There are different stages that a woman goes through in her sexual life. There is the young and sometimes wild stage of exploring and risk taking. There is the more mature stage where depth and monogamy are important. There is the possible stage where a woman is pregnant, nursing or has little children underfoot, and time and sensitivity are deeply needed. There is the stage of career, where time and focus are important. There is also the stage of menopause and post menopause, where understanding and sensitivity must be present. Or a woman can be in a combination of these different stages. But in all of these stages, a woman likes to be invited into the sexual experience in a loving and beautiful way. No matter what stage she is in, a little extra care on the part of the man can open her heart and body to the sexual experience.

When we had our first daughter, we needed to adjust our sexual life a bit. We had been together for eleven years before Rami was born and were used to being spontaneous in our decision to make love. The presence of a nursing baby changed the spontaneity but, with care and sensitivity, did not diminish the beauty of the experience. Barry learned to adjust his schedule on a certain day so that we both could be available when our baby napped. Sometimes she would only sleep for one hour, so we needed to use that time well. I normally cleaned up the kitchen for part of that time when she slept. So while I nursed her to sleep, Barry cleaned up the kitchen or did whatever household chores needed doing so I could feel really free and relaxed during this one hour while she slept. Yes, cleaning the kitchen can be an important part of foreplay!

As we added two more children, we had to keep adjusting. With three children to care for and guide, I found my thoughts spinning around their needs, and our sexual needs could easily be put way down on my priority list. By the time all three children were in bed at night, I was often exhausted. Because we spaced our children over thirteen years, there was a young one around for many years. Barry decided that, if he wanted to have beautiful lovemaking with me, he needed to do something about the children. All on his own, he arranged childcare during the day or overnight, and drove the children to the different friends' homes, or arranged after-school care. It was a lot of effort on his part to have time alone with me. But that act of taking care of the children's needs himself, rather than my always having to do it, was very attractive to me. It wouldn't have worked if I had to ask or remind him to take care of the children's needs. Taking the initiative on his own was Barry's way of inviting me, at that stage of my life, into the sexual experience. Being alone in the house was a wonderful luxury that we both enjoyed tremendously.

Preparing a Romantic Atmosphere

I have always enjoyed when Barry lights candles, or brings in flowers, or puts on lovely music to make the space more beautiful and inviting. One woman told how her husband would clean the room, then light aromatic candles and gently invite her into the room. This was attractive to her. Another woman told how her husband would fill a bath with warm, scented water and then light candles around the bath. He would invite her to relax in the tub while he put the children to sleep. She knew he had a motive for this luxury, but it was still charming to her. One woman told me that she likes it when her husband takes her out to dinner and hires a babysitter to put the children to bed. Over dinner, she and her husband can have a fulfilling, uninterrupted conversation. Often, but not always, the mood for lovemaking is present when they return home.

Preparing a romantic atmosphere for a close, sexual experience is important to a woman, and a way for a man to show his love. It may seem like a lot of effort and time, but the rewards of taking the time to properly invite a woman into the experience are completely worth it. By sensitively inviting a woman into physical intimacy, you are opening the door for her to pour her love and sensuality into you. No amount of time or effort can possibly be too much to receive her precious gift of love and sexual energy.

*I feel so loved by you Aaron when I come home,
walk into the room, and your whole body lights
up. You are ready to grab me and overwhelm
me with your love, yet you wait and let me walk
up to you and give you a kiss.*
–Suzanne Nitzkin, Long Beach, CA

Taking Time for Lovemaking

Barry: For Joyce, making love is like a gourmet stew cooked in a slow cooker, not a microwave oven or a pressure cooker. For her, real lovemaking requires lots of time and no pressure. Our ideal is to give ourselves as much time as possible, with minimal work in the office, or other stresses. Like so many other people, we carry many responsibilities on our shoulders, so many things to do. Over the years we have realized that the world doesn't stop spinning when we take a day off. Our email in-box just gets a little (or a lot) fuller, the phone messages increase somewhat, but it all can wait. Joyce and I deserve to nurture our relationship. In fact, we now feel that nurturing ourselves and each other is what the world needs most from us. We love being of service in the world, and have found that nurturing our own relationship is a powerful way to be of service.

On this day off, I encourage Joyce to take as much quality personal time alone as she needs. Being a more inward person, she thrives on this alone time. Even though I am more of an extrovert, I still need time alone just as much. If we don't give first to ourselves, how can we expect to really give to one another?

Ideally, we spend enough quality time with each other before our time of lovemaking. Sharing vulnerably, and being heard by the other, allows a deeper intimacy ("into me see"). Our goal is intimacy, not sex. The vulnerability and connection *are* the lovemaking. They may or may not lead to sex, and this is accepted and understood by both of us.

After our personal time, I enjoy preparing our bedroom. I light candles, and then put on our favorite romantic music.

Sacred Sexuality

If it becomes clear that we're ready for our bodies to enter the lovemaking, I know that Joyce wants a joining of our souls, a shared spiritual time. We hold each other, give thanks, and ask to feel and celebrate the joining of our bodies, hearts and souls. Foreplay is much more than physical. This is spiritual and emotional foreplay. Perhaps we should rename this "forepray."

It's important for me to say that physical sex – or orgasm – is never the goal. This takes so much pressure off us both. Our goal is always to feel love, to give and to receive the highest gifts, rather than having an orgasm. Making love is so much deeper than the physical act. Rather than a destination, it is a journey of discovery.

Joyce loves when I kiss her lips, but she also loves my spoken words of appreciation and adoration. Joyce's physical touch turns me on, but it's my loving words as well as my touch that turn her on the most. She melts when I massage her back, and take a luxuriantly long time doing it. And she melts even more when I tell her all that I love about her during the back rub.

> *Joyce, you are a divine goddess. Your smile lights up any room. Your eyes bathe me with tender love. Your hands not only touch my body, they touch my deepest places within. Your voice is the essence of music, even sweeter than music. Your body is the most beautiful body in the world. No actress, no model, can have a more perfect body than you. And when I look into your eyes, I see divine woman, ageless woman, woman who defines the concept of beauty.*

I am careful to move slowly, and touch lightly, as well as be touched, but not too much. Too much stimulation causes me to get too excited, more genital-centered than heart-centered, and then I leave Joyce behind. She, like most women, is much slower to warm up sexually. As I continue to mature, I find that I actually need just as much time as Joyce. Yes, I can have an orgasm in a few minutes, but that's just physical sex, and has little to do with making love. We all have a spiritual-emotional body as well as a physical body. And this subtle body needs much more time, gentleness, and love to become fully aroused. Fast food may fill your belly, but a gourmet meal fills your soul as well as your belly.

I sometimes place my hand over her heart and send my love through my hand into her heart. This feels so good to me as well as Joyce, and I let her know that I am doing this, and what I am feeling. Or I place one hand on her heart and one hand on her pubic area, sending love to both areas, and I ask her to let the energy from both my hands enter both heart and genitals, and then join together, connecting both areas … uniting love with sexuality … creating sacred sexuality.

Most important, I wait for her – not a passive or impatient waiting – but an extremely enjoyable waiting, watching and feeling her open like a flower. Joyce's sensual blossoming is so enjoyable that my own experience, my own arousal and sensations, while still delicious, pale in comparison. I reassure her that her taking a longer time to warm up sexually is not something I patiently endure. Rather, her slowness is an enormous gift to me that helps me to slow down, to have my heart catch up to my body, and to become fully attuned to her heart.

Joyce's natural inclination, like many women, is to give to me, to make sure I am sexually fulfilled, but sometimes at her own expense. She can easily sacrifice her own sexual arousal to yield to my experience. It's her giving and nurturing nature, similar to most women. Whereas, I become more aroused and feel my sensuality more *when I give to her.* Therefore, the more I can relieve her of any responsibility to take care of me sexually, the more she can relax into her own sexuality. It's important for me to also gently give her permission to have times of not giving to me during lovemaking – to just completely let go and feel the light of God fill every cell of her body. I give her permission to enter into her Goddess-Self, and receive my complete adoration. For it is precisely her receptivity that fills my heart to overflowing, at the same time driving me wild with passion.

If it becomes clear that we are moving together toward a climax, we stop one last time for a special prayer. Joyce likes me to speak out loud something like this:

> *Beloved God (Presence, Spirit, Light, etc.), help us to join in our hearts and souls as we now join with our bodies. And allow this joining to bless all the world with light.*

Even in this delicious and powerful time immediately before orgasm, the conscious intention to join spiritually and bathe the world in the light of our union, allows a heightening of the orgasm, a more deeply shared ecstasy. Two of us joining during orgasm is sublime. The whole universe joining within and around us goes far beyond any words can describe. For us, this is the essence of sacred sexuality.

Keeping my eyes open allows me to remain more conscious. Looking into Joyce's sparkling blue eyes allows me to continue our divine connection, even during orgasm.

Sex doesn't end after orgasm. Far from it, this is the time for us to bask in the luminous afterglow of two hearts joining. Joyce loves it when I hold her and thank her for the privilege of being with her, of adoring her, and being the object of her adoration. I stay with her afterwards as long as she wants. The energy of our lovemaking stays with us, perhaps not as powerfully, but still there. We kiss, hug, and appreciate one another. Sometimes we have some of our deepest talks after making love. We have been blessed by divine lovemaking.

Joyce recently shared with me that she can feel pulsations in her vagina sometimes even hours after making love. These sensations keep the energy of lovemaking alive. Although we may no longer be in bed, we are in a way still making love. This awareness has helped me to remain sensitive to her in the waking hours after lovemaking. Business decisions or other stressful conversations just have to wait until later.

To Really Love a Woman's Body

Barry and I want to emphasize that loving, honoring, and appreciating your beloved woman's body is a powerful, beautiful and sustaining way to show your love. All women, regardless of their age or size, enjoy having their body seen as beautiful by the man they love. This is a special way to love her, as long as you don't *only* focus on her body. Women also need to be appreciated for their inner qualities. Women need to be seen as a whole person, not just a beautiful body. But as long as you are appreciating her as a whole person, then appreciating her body will be seen as deeply honoring.

In our American culture, we, as women, are constantly being bombarded by the near impossible model of perfection. In the movies, we see actresses with "perfect" bodies, hair, make-up and skin. Standing in the grocery or drug store line, we can't help but see all the magazines with "perfect" looking actresses and models on the covers. How can we possibly compare to these women, who have had make-up artists, hairdressers and photographers make them look flawless? We can say to ourself, "Well, it's just the make-up that makes them look that way." But inside every woman, if even just a tiny bit, she physically compares herself, and comes out inferior to these "perfect" models of women.

In the almost forty years of doing workshops and counseling women, I have yet to meet a woman who feels that her body is beautiful enough. There always seems to be some fault that she is not at peace with. Once, at a week-long retreat we were leading, there was a young woman who I assumed was completely at peace with her physical appearance. Molly had what the media would consider a perfect body, along with gorgeous, long, curly blond hair and deep blue eyes. She was a singer with a strong, powerful voice. In the middle of the week, we led a process in which people shared in small groups how they had difficulty loving their body. The workshop participants were going quite deep in this process.

Toward the end, Molly took her turn. Soon the room was filled with deep crying. Molly was expressing more pain than any of the other participants. I rushed over to be with her. She kept saying, "I am such a fake!" She pointed at her breasts and lips and told how she had had them altered, so they would be more perfect. Her hair was not her natural color, and it took her over an hour each day to put on her make-up. She wore blue contacts on her eyes. Through deep crying and grief, she told how she never allowed herself to enjoy eating and was always dieting in order to keep her figure the way it was. Molly shared, "I am so afraid to just be myself. I am so afraid that men wouldn't accept me if I was just my natural self. I want to let go of all this fakeness and just be me."

With the help of the group, we encouraged Molly to not wear her make-up for the remainder of the week, to wear her clear contact lenses, and to enjoy the meals and eat the way she wanted. We all appreciated Molly in her more natural state. She truly looked better to all of us. She left the retreat a happier woman.

I am sharing all this so you will realize that a woman needs her physical appearance to be loved and appreciated in its natural form. This is such a beautiful gift that you can give her. It feels so wonderful to a woman to know that you really love her body and find her attractive.

Barry has loved my body in all of its changes throughout our years together. He has always let me know that he finds me attractive and is turned on to me. With much enthusiasm, Barry tells me over and over again that I am the most attractive woman to him. His appreciations of my body touch me deeply. No matter what physical change I am going through, Barry seems to take delight in it.

I always had a thin body, until I became pregnant with our first child. Three months into the pregnancy, I didn't feel pregnant, just overweight. My stomach was round and sticking out. I didn't like looking like that. I mentioned my discomfort with my looks to Barry one morning before I got dressed. He told me he had never seen me look more beautiful. He began kissing my belly and saying how sexy I looked. I felt anything but sexy, but his enthusiasm was so genuine that soon I began to feel that my new look was beautiful. As the baby grew within me, Barry could hardly keep his hands off of me, saying he thought all the changes in my body made me so attractive and sexy. It was hard to be self-absorbed in how much weight I was gaining, when his enthusiasm for how I looked was so prevalent. After Rami was born, it took a while for my figure to return. I also had big breasts that seemed to leak in the most inopportune times, getting my clothes all wet. Barry loved all these changes. He kept telling me that he was so attracted to me, and found me more beautiful than ever.

When I went through menopause, Barry continued to love me through all the changes. In Barry's presence I really feel like the most attractive woman in his eyes. This has been such an amazing gift that he has given to me. Because he is so appreciative of my body, I am naturally so open to him physically. I feel safe and completely welcome into his arms.

Wanting Only Her

A woman needs to know that she is more desirable to her partner than anyone or anything else. A woman needs to know that her partner wants only her. Nothing kills the feeling of safety for a woman than when her partner turns to other women or pornography for sexual pleasure. Having an affair with another is perhaps the hardest thing to overcome in a relationship. It is difficult for a woman or man to feel honored and loved when their partner has had sex with someone else. Many relationships do not survive an affair and, if they do, it takes years to regain the trust.

Many men feel that pornography is okay, because they are not actually having sex with a real woman. These men rationalize their actions by asserting that all men use pornography. The answer is that men who value their beloved will not use porn. Porn and a good relationship do not go together. We have never seen a good relationship where the man also uses porn. Porn is a direct insult to the woman. By looking at nude women, many of them still teenagers, the man is saying that these are the bodies that turn him on. His partner then feels in second place, or not as attractive as the pictures or videos. It feels like the man is having an affair with other people, even though they are in the form of images. She may not let you know how much this hurts her, but she will also not be as open to you physically because she will not feel completely safe with you.

To love and honor her, let her know that she is the most attractive woman to you and that no one or no image is more beautiful than her natural self. Let her know every day, in many different ways, how attractive she is to you. Some women spend considerable time dressing and doing their hair for a dinner date with their husband, and the guy doesn't even notice. To really love her, notice how she looks and let her know that she is the most beautiful woman in the restaurant in your eyes. These are ways that keep the romance alive, even after many years. She will respond with love and openness to you.

Sometimes I try to imagine what it will be like when Barry and I are both in our nineties. I picture myself the way my mother looked at age eighty-nine, wrinkled and gray. I also picture Barry by my side telling me that I am still attractive to him, and to him I am still the most beautiful woman in the room. I imagine smiling at him and loving him with all my heart, because I will know that he is not just saying that. He will really still mean it. I am his Goddess and the knowledge of that causes such an opening of my heart to him.

> *As I get older and my breasts are sagging, and I'm growing wrinkles and gray hair, Rob continues to adore my body, and wants me.*
> – Karla Gitlin, Redwood Valley, CA

Woman's Night

Leslie and James, a couple in their early thirties, described a deep love and caring in their relationship, except in their sex life. James wished Leslie would enjoy sex more, would be more attracted to him, and would be more sexually spontaneous. Leslie felt that, most of the time, sex was about James – his needs, his wishes, even his orgasm. Although she felt James's love for her at other times, during sex she mostly felt his desire for her body. She didn't really feel loved and cherished. And most of the time, this was actually fine with her. She was happy that James was getting what he needed. She was happy to give herself to him. But sometimes she wished he could give to her what she needed.

James felt sad about these statements. He wanted to be a considerate lover and partner. And he was confused. He turned to us and said, "I get so attracted to Leslie, and swept away with my feelings. What am I doing wrong?"

Because of James and Leslie, and many other couples in the same situation, we have come up with a solution: "Woman's Night." At least one night a week, we explained to James, it is Leslie's night. It doesn't even need to be a night. It can be any time during the day. But it has to be Leslie's time, where *her* needs are considered, *her* feelings are listened to, *her* eyes are looked into, and *her* body is not touched with desire. The block of time, however long, is all about *her*.

We asked Leslie and James, "Are you willing to work hard to create an ecstatic, sensual, and deeply fulfilling sexual relationship?" They both answered yes.

We told James, "At least once a week, make it clear that this time is all about her, and not about your sex drive, your genitals, or her body. Show her your interest in her thoughts, feelings, dreams and desires. Let her know that you value her for much more than her body. Let her know how important she is to you, her friendship, her love, her motherhood, and her little girl inside. Let her know the ways you are proud of her, and especially, continually remind her that she deserves to be treated as special, that she deserves to receive your abundant love and cherishing. If she wants, touch or massage her body as a way of giving your love, your blessing, your healing, without any genital or sexual contact. If you become aroused, your gift to both yourself and to Leslie is to not have to do anything about your erection, your sexual desire, your needs. Touch her body as a way to touch her soul, rather than as a way to get your own needs met. "

Then we told Leslie, "This is your time to be divinely selfish, in other words, selfish in a good and necessary way. It's your time to practice receiving, to really learn the art of receiving love from your mate, knowing that you fully deserve it. However, the requirement is your honest requests for what you need, and your honest responses to James's words and actions. This is not about taking care of James. It's about your own honesty and needs. That's your challenge. Even though you want him to be a mind reader, sometimes he's not. If he says something that feels good, let him know. If he says something that's not helpful, rather than criticize him, try instead to gently ask for what you need. Same with touching. If it feels good, tell him. Even if his touches slightly feel 'him-oriented,' it won't work for you to lie there and hope he realizes his shift in focus. Again, as considerately as you can, ask for what you need. Yes, of course, you're teaching him the subtle art of love-making – but this is different from taking care of his needs at your own expense."

Some couples may be reversed, where it's the woman's needs that are dominating the relationship and the man who is the caretaker. In this case, a "man's night" may be what is needed.

Men, you may be tempted to treat "woman's night" as a way of scoring points with your woman. You may have the secret thought, "If I patiently listen to her for an hour, or share my innermost thoughts and feelings, or touch her the way she wants, then she'll give me what I want." This will always backfire. She will not feel your love. She'll only feel your desire.

Women, you may be tempted to receive your partner's unselfish love for only a short time, as if to say, "I only deserve a little love." Then you may give up on yourself and give in to your partner's needs. This, too, will backfire, because you will feel cheated and resentful, and will in some way take it out on both of you.

Both of you deserve fulfilling love – and fulfilling sex. Both of you deserve to receive generously and equally from each other. Both of you deserve to teach and to learn from one another.

Sexual Moments

Joseph and Samantha took our advice. No matter how busy they felt they were, every Saturday starting at 5pm was their date night. Both self-employed, they previously had trouble setting limits on their work schedule. They would typically plan a special time together, only to let some unplanned deadline swallow it up. Ever since they made their commitment to their weekly date, their relationship took an upswing. Sometimes they went out to dinner, sometimes a show, sometimes dancing, sometimes just a long walk. Almost always, a special part of their date was coming back home to make love.

Now, six months later, they faced another challenge. Sex was losing its magic, its spontaneity. It only happened on Saturday night. The rest of the week seemed to be lost in a blur of frenetic activity and ever-demanding work.

We asked Samantha and Joseph, "What about the little passionate moments that are possible throughout the day, like long kisses or hugs, or a moment for a deeper appreciation rather than a simple compliment, or the intimacy of looking into one another's eyes, or even a brief massage?"

Joseph's response surprised me. He said, "I don't want to start anything I can't finish. If I kiss Samantha longer than a few seconds, I might start to feel sexually aroused, and it might not be a good time for Samantha to make love."

Samantha nodded in agreement and piped in, "Isn't it unhealthy for a man to have an erection and then not use it?"

The answer is a definitive no. Erections come and go with no physical ill effects. As men, the problem is our own psychological (not physiological) attachment to our orgasms. Whether it is our selfish desire for pleasure or our feeling of what it is to be a "real" man, this is *not* how to love a woman. If she agrees to have a sexual moment with you, and you get carried away by your own needs, you have then, in a way, left her. You love her best by catching yourself when your mind leaves your brain and enters your genitals. You love her by saying something like, "Wow, I'm really getting into this! Would you like to stop now and maybe resume at another time?" And you love her by honoring her request to stop at any time, and let yourself cool down, rather than whining or begging for more.

Joyce and I are amazed at how many couples cringe at the thought of a sexual moment. This is an archaic view of sexuality. There is no starting or ending point in our sexual relationship. Conscious sex neither starts with physical arousal nor ends with an orgasm. It cannot be artificially separated from the rest of our relationship. Sensual or sexual moments are delightful gifts even in the midst of the busiest of days. Tapping into sexual feelings keeps the spark of love alive, fans those warm embers, and makes wonderful reminders.

We told Joseph and Samantha that sex doesn't have to be in a box, isolated to one part of their busy schedule. Sexual energy is an integral part of the relationship, part of the loving connection. Sexual moments can happen at any time of the day, and don't need to be anything more than a moment. If a long kiss leads to arousal ... wonderful. Learn to enjoy the moment of arousal as a complete moment, rather than seeing it as a step toward intercourse. That way, when you do fully make love, it will be as if your sexuality is a continuum, rather than an isolated event in time. And it's this continuity, the stringing together of even little sexual moments, that allows lovemaking to be truly magical.

When Joyce and I participate in sexual moments throughout the day, kisses longer than usual, caresses or holding, our sexual energies don't go dormant. We love to take walks on our local beach with our golden retrievers. The dogs can run free, chasing birds through the surf. From time to time we stop for a sexual moment, especially when there's nobody around. We enjoy a sexual appetizer, with kisses and touches opening our erotic energies. Sure, my brain may take a dip into a lower chakra, and I might not want to stop. And yes, I may bulge even uncomfortably, and even suggest we go up against the cliff where we can be more alone. But we have a clear agreement. This is only a sexual moment, an appetizer rather than a whole meal. Either one of us (okay, usually Joyce) can ask to resume walking. However uncomfortable it is to walk, eventually the bulge subsides, and we are left with a delightful re-freshing feeling in our bodies and newly invigorated minds.

Joseph and Samantha were delighted. This seemed to be a whole new territory for them. Samantha looked at Joseph, a twinkle in her eyes, and said, "I just want to make sure, Joseph, that you can eat an appetizer without wanting the whole meal to immediately follow."

Joseph smiled and said, "I never knew I had permission to just eat an appetizer."

Samantha and Joseph are doing just fine. They report much more closeness and intimacy, and tell us their Saturday night dates have been exquisite.

> *It always amazes me that, after 15 years of marriage, if my husband is wanting or needing skin to skin contact with my breast or other vulnerable parts of me, always, without fail, he asks first.*
> –Gail Swain, Watsonville, CA

Please Just Hold Me!

Marty and Sheila were stuck. And they were stuck like many couples we have seen in counseling sessions and workshops. Sex wasn't working. Marty was feeling sexually frustrated, continually disappointed in Sheila's lack of interest in sex. A picture was being painted of Sheila with a problem of sexual dysfunction.

We asked Sheila what she needed. She thought for a moment, then replied, "I just need to be held by Marty." It was hard for Sheila to say that, just like it is hard for many people to give voice to their deeper need. Many women feel guilty about their need for non-sexual touch, that there's something wrong with them for not being instantly sexually available to their partner like in the movies. There may also be the old programming that says a woman needs to be available to please her mate. But for so many women, there is a deep need to experience the love of a father, the safe, non-pressuring nurturing that simply lets her be who she is. It's not that Sheila was against having sex with Marty. She in fact expressed strong feelings of attraction for him. Their relationship had simply progressed to the point where Sheila's deeper needs were coming to the surface, and she could no longer suppress them.

What about Marty's frustration? For Marty, as with many men, the sexual act was the main, if not the only, way he gave and received nurturing in the relationship. He needed to learn how to give and receive love in other, non-sexual ways, for example, through active and compassionate listening, through sharing his inner self and more vulnerable feelings, and through non-sexual touch and holding. A key for Marty, and for many men, is the awareness of his own need for the nurturing of a mother. It is natural for little boys to transition from total dependence upon their mothers to a pushing-away stage of growth in an attempt toward self-reliance. But eventually all boys need to come to terms with their need for the nurturing love of the mother. It is really the nurturing love of the mother-father, or parent energy. It is somewhat artificial to separate parental nurturing into one or another sex.

So, for Marty to open to his need for this parental love, which can come through Sheila, he will become more vulnerable to her. As he allows himself to be held and nurtured as a child, he becomes able to hold and nurture Sheila's inner child. In other words, as he accepts the deeper needs of his own inner child, he is allowed to accept similar needs in another.

Sheila needs to give a clear and guilt-free voice to her inner child. She needs to know it is right to need non-sexual nurturing. As she understands the acceptability of her soul-level needs, she will be able to communicate them more clearly ... without anger, withdrawal, depression or however else these unaccepted feelings come to the surface.

When there is enough non-sexual expression of caring in a relationship, then the sexual expression can be more fulfilling. When the soul, and the inner child, feel safe and nurtured, then the body is freed to feel the highest levels of ecstasy.

When we first met, I had been experiencing severe insomnia for a number of years. I was touched but skeptical about my new boyfriend's promise "to give me good sleep." But EVERY night for the last 3 years, we "assume" our position with my head lying on his chest, while Richard tenderly massages my shoulders, neck, face or scalp until we both drift off. Should I wake up restless later in the night, he again invites me to "assume the position" and despite his own fatigue, lovingly strokes me back to sleep. Though my insomnia is not yet totally banished, I am happier, more rested and energetic than I've been in years and so grateful for my now husband's thoughtful and generous loving.

–Ann Rickard, Kapoho, HI

Is it Sex or Love?

I have spoken to many men who admit that sex is their way to love. The physical act of sex helps them to open their hearts to connect with their partners, whereas many women need heart connection first so they can be open to sex. Many couples, therefore, are truly stuck. He wants sex in order to feel love. She wants love in order to enjoy sex.

To really love a woman, you can't use her body to meet your own needs. Even if it helps you to feel love, she may still feel used. There is an addictive element to this kind of sex. It's using sex as a kind of drug to help fill a void. If there is even the slightest pressure put on her, whether it's to have sex in the first place, or to do certain things during sex, love goes out the window. Pressure and love cannot coexist. "Pressure" is wanting something from her. "Love" is wanting to give something to her.

So many times have I put sexual pressure on Joyce, thinking I was loving her. So many times have I approached sex from a place of emptiness needing to be filled, rather than fullness needing to give love. So many times during lovemaking have I pressured Joyce into doing something she didn't feel comfortable doing.

Okay, there is a place for "casual sex." There can be a time for "me sex" rather than "you sex." It's about consensus – both of you agreeing to something ahead of time. But if she feels used by you, even a little, something will be taken away from the relationship. If it's more "me sex" than "you sex," it's more getting than giving, and the relationship becomes unbalanced.

To really love a woman, you need to learn how to open your heart to love – before you have sex. To really love her, you need to learn how to fill your own cup of love first. Perhaps it's the journey of a lifetime, but it's the first steps that make all the difference. If you're willing especially to start and maintain an emotional-spiritual healing journey, to learn to really love yourself rather than merely paying lip service to it, she will notice. So much pressure to be your source of love will be taken off her. It truly makes her happy when she feels you taking care of yourself spiritually and emotionally. She is sensitive to the difference between your advances out of love and your advances out of need.

We sometimes lead circle dances in our retreats. Sometimes, in couple's retreats, we'll break up into a circle of men outside a circle of women. We deliberately focus on the men and women connecting with the others in their own circle. When the women's circle silently watches the men connecting in brotherhood, we consistently hear the same comments. Each woman delights in the lack of pressure on them to be the source of love for their man.

Find the joy of giving pleasure to her as an end in itself, not as a precursor to having her give you pleasure back. Find the ecstasy in the experience of giving itself. What I love most about making love with Joyce are those moments when she is not doing anything for me. Yes, she loves me most wonderfully in her receptivity. It sends me to the heights of bliss when I feel her body open fully like a flower. I see her face and body as the most divinely sensual earth goddess. My own sexual feelings pale in comparison to this love-burst. Time stands still in these moments of serving the goddess, of worshipping the one divine presence sharing bodies with her and me. If only it could never end!

Sexual Communication: What You Appreciate

Sacred sexuality starts with the desire to bring more love into your sexuality. In our couple's workshops, we have each person communicate with their partner about sexuality in two ways.

First, we invite them to appreciate or acknowledge something beautiful about their sexual relationship. There is perhaps no area of relationship that needs appreciation more. Some of the deepest wounds in relationship have occurred because of sexual criticism, or comparing someone unfavorably with a previous partner. There is always something good to be appreciated. Most couples simply don't take the time to acknowledge the goodness of their sexuality as a couple, or the goodness of their partner's sexuality.

Each of you take as much time as you need to appreciate the beauty of any part of your sexual

relationship or your partner's sexuality. Take
turns with this, each of you addressing one
thing at a time. Remember specific times of
lovemaking that were special. Describe to your
lover the specific things they did that really
turned you on. Once you begin this dialogue,
you may not want it to end. That's how important it is.

Sexual Communication: What You Need

Now let your lover know what you need to be
more deeply fulfilled sexually. This is not an opportunity to tell your partner what they are doing wrong. Rather, it is a time to give vital information about yourself to your partner.
Please be sensitive. There are certain things
your lover may not feel comfortable doing. This
is not a time to put pressure on them to do what
you want.
If you want, start the practice by completing a
statement like this:
It really turns me on when you _____.
I feel really loved when you _____.

Challenges to Sexually Loving a Woman

LIFE CAN PRESENT OBSTACLES TO MAKING LOVE TO A WOMAN. But no obstacle is too big to be surmounted if there is enough love and persistence.

The Two Sides of Impotence

Let's look at impotence. Impotence may be medically or psychologically attributed to one partner, but it cannot be overcome unless both partners take responsibility for each of their own parts. If one partner is blamed for impotence, then the "hidden impotence" of the other partner continues the dysfunction in the relationship.

Here's an example: Eliza blamed John for his impotence in their relationship. And John blamed himself as well. Looking only at the surface, it makes sense. John couldn't keep his erection. How could that have anything to do with Eliza? In our counseling sessions with them, we noticed that John was blamed for more than only unsatisfactory sex. In fact, he was blamed for everything that wasn't working in their relationship. He didn't make enough money. He didn't talk enough about his feelings. He wasn't spiritual enough.

When we asked Eliza to take responsibility for her own unhealthy contribution to their relationship, she first looked perplexed, then annoyed with us. She was, after all, an innocent victim, and she was unwilling to see that this position was her own "impotence." Blaming John for all the problems not only kept her from working on herself, but it kept her small and weak, in other words, impotent.

During one session, Joyce and I kept bringing the attention back to Eliza. We asked questions about her childhood. Eliza was, naturally, resistant to look at her own issues. But we gently persisted. When we finally saw tears in her eyes, we knew we were on track. We asked, "What are the tears about, Eliza?"

"There is something, but I don't want to talk about it."

We didn't say anything. We knew she just needed a little time.

With her eyes still closed, she finally said, "My mother did the same thing to my father!"

"What did she do?"

"The same thing I'm doing. My mother blamed everything on my father. She complained about him constantly to me. It hurt me so much because I knew some of the things were her fault. When I tried to speak up on his behalf, she always got angry at me, so I just stopped. I gave up on the truth. I stopped standing up for my father. And he still doesn't stand up for himself."

She started sobbing, while John, who had never seen his wife be so vulnerable, put his arm around her and pulled her close.

She let herself be held for a while, then sat back to look into his eyes and said, "I'm so sorry, John. I never understood how messed up my childhood was. I've hated the part of my mother that is so critical of my father, and I've turned out to be just like her. Now I hate that part of myself."

Her sobbing continued, and John pulled her close. She collapsed into his loving arms.

And yes, their relationship changed quickly after that session. Eliza learned how to recognize her lack of self-love, rather than blaming John. John learned to stand up more for himself. And the sexual relationship? Now that two people were working on their impotence – dramatically improved!

"Frigidity"

Then there's so-called "frigidity." Because her father sexually molested Minnie as a child, Derrick blamed her for the scarcity of lovemaking in their relationship. He expressed anger at her father for ruining her life, and making his life so much harder. He was frustrated by how many conditions Minnie placed on their sexual life. It could only happen in the evening, when the room was completely dark. She was uncomfortable being seen naked. She didn't like Derrick touching her breasts or genitals. Only one position was acceptable: her on top, so she could be more in control.

We asked Derrick about any sexual wounds from his past, and he quickly denied any. Perhaps too quickly. So we had to slow him down and ask specific questions about his early life.

Joyce and I understand that no one gets through childhood and, especially, adolescence, without any sexual trauma. It may not be incest or molestation, but these are not the only ways we are damaged sexually.

Minnie finally volunteered a key piece of information about Derrick. When he was about eight years old, he and his best friend experimented sexually with each other.

"What exactly did you do with each other," we asked.

"I'd rather not talk about it," was Derrick's quick reply.

But he looked uncomfortable.

While he sat there squirming, we told him, "What you did as an eight-year-old is probably entirely normal."

"No it wasn't," Derrick blurted out. "It was a sin."

"Okay, then give us a chance as your counselors to help you with this."

A long pause, and then, "He touched my penis and I touched his. It was wrong! I never should've allowed it to happen. All through my teen years I worried that I might be gay. I never told anyone about it, except Minnie one time."

In that moment he looked like he was carrying a huge weight on his shoulders.

"Sorry, Derrick. Eight-year-olds sometimes need to explore."

Derrick at first looked surprised, then he took a deep, slow breath and we felt the weight lifting off his shoulders. Minnie placed her hand tenderly on top of his hand.

He looked at his wife and said, "I just didn't understand my part until now. I've been so focused on what your father did to you. I didn't realize how much I've been carrying."

Once again, now that there are two people who understand their own sexual challenges, they can work together as a team to heal them.

Aging

As Joyce and I are aging, there are unique challenges in our own sexual relationship. In my younger years, I rarely had a problem maintaining an erection for long and lingering lovemaking. Currently, I want our lovemaking to last even longer, to really savor it as a gourmet feast. But I can't do this without paying close attention to my senior body. Like running a marathon, I have to pace myself. Unlike running a marathon, the finish line is not as important as the joy of running. Well, maybe for some runners...

I have to pay more attention to the buildup of sexual energy. If I get too close to orgasm, even if I stop at this point, I sometimes feel a release of energy that I can describe as a partial orgasm. It's extremely pleasurable, but without ejaculation. My sexual energy then dissipates, along with my erection. Joyce has become aware of this new phenomenon, and accepts and loves me when this happens. I do sometimes feel a little disappointed in myself, even though Joyce does not feel let down. We talk about what just happened. Sometimes we laugh about it. Always, I let go of any disappointment and we continue to cuddle and love one another, which is, after all, the real goal. The physical part of sex may be over, but the lovemaking continues.

Because of the possibility of a partial orgasm, here's what I do. I concentrate even more on giving sexually to Joyce. This is wonderful for me! The more pleasure I can give to her, the more pleasure I feel.

I more closely monitor the actions that heighten my arousal too much, such as penetration. It is best for both of us when I do not enter Joyce until we are both ready for orgasm. I want to stay with her. The more I am *with* her, the deeper my pleasure. In other words, especially with my genitals, less is more; a little touch goes a long way. I make sure I stop movement periodically to look into Joyce's eyes, to adore her with my words, or to sing to her (she loves it when I sing to her). If there's one thing we've learned about sex: it's impossible to go too slow!

We communicate. We experiment. We find new ways to give and receive love.

The important thing is to find what works for both of you.

In *To Really Love a Man,* we told part of Donna and Ron Sturm's story. After his prostate cancer surgery, Donna made love to Ron even though he was unable to have an erection. She initiated sex even though he had no desire. She refused to give up on their sexual relationship.

But after a while of giving her love to Ron, Donna began to ask herself, "What if the tables were turned, and I was unable to feel or perform sexually? I wouldn't let that stop me from giving pleasure to Ron."

That afternoon, after a few minutes cuddling in bed, she popped up on one elbow and said, "Ron, there's something I need to ask you."

"What's that," was Ron's concerned reply.

"I know you feel practically no sexual feelings right now because of the female hormones you're taking. And I certainly don't want you to stop taking them if they help you stay cancer-free. But I desire you sexually. I need you to touch me, kiss me, and love me. I know you can't use your penis right now, but I want you to use your hands and mouth on my body."

Ron described his process at that point, "At first I had no idea what to do. So much of my concept of sexuality was centered in my penis. But it obviously wasn't working. Without my own arousal and desire, how could I give pleasure to Donna? This, I realized, was my own self-centeredness. I had no choice in that moment. To love Donna,

I must forget about my own physical pleasure, and just give to her.

"And that's what I did. I caressed her body. I kissed her body. Without my own sexual desire getting in the way, I was amazed at how sensitive I could be. I could somehow feel the full subtleties of her pleasure in my own body. When she finally reached a climax, it was the most incredible feeling for me as well. It was like I reached a climax too, but not one that brought an end to the buildup of sexual energy. Rather it was a wonderful feeling of love in every part of my body and soul, a feeling that lasted as we held one another in a sacred embrace. It felt like a spiritual, rather than just a physical, orgasm."

The Myth of Penis Size

In one study, 63% of men thought their penis was too small. Not one of them was smaller than average. That's almost two thirds of men who suffer needlessly from "Small Penis Syndrome."

In another study, it was found that larger than average penis size actually correlated with a lack of orgasm in their female partner.

It was also found that most women who complained about the small penis size of their partner, were women who could not orgasm during sex. They were trying to blame something for their lack of satisfaction.

What about the few men who actually have a smaller than average penis? Penis size has never prevented a woman from being satisfied sexually. It's not how big your penis is; it's how it's used that matters most. And far more than the penis, sexually satisfying a woman, as you have read in this section of the book, is more about your heart and expressing your love.

Men are actually no different than women when it comes to body image. The ads and billboards don't only show the idealized female body. We suffer with the same feelings of inadequacy or ugliness. Unique to men, however, is a cultivated judgment about smallness in a masculine world where bigness is the goal. A small man has more to overcome than a small woman. Small boys are picked on more often than small girls. Big muscles are seen as more manly. And so is a bigger penis.

We all started out small as babies, then children, then teens. The problem is especially acute as teens, where older teens poked fun at younger teens in high school locker rooms. I remember an especially painful time as a freshman. An older boy with a significantly larger penis was parading around the locker room, laughing at the younger boys like me, spreading shame wherever he walked.

I'll say it again: the size of your penis does not matter at all! *If a woman feels loved by you, it's your love, more than your penis, that brings her pleasure.* If you focus your full attention on bringing her pleasure with your penis, and fail to connect with her, lover to lover, you will not succeed regardless of the size of your penis.

Ron in the previous section, who had no use of his penis because of his prostate cancer and surgery, learned an even more fulfilling way to satisfy his wife. He learned how to make love with Donna.

Becoming Vulnerable with a Woman

TO BE VULNERABLE WITH YOUR BELOVED IS TO AL-
LOW YOURSELF TO BE SEEN AND KNOWN IN YOUR EN-
TIRETY, not just your powerful, independent, secure, loving and capable self. To be vulnerable is to show her your
fear, pain, shame, and need for love. Showing your vulnerability, by definition, is showing your weakness and therefore showing the way to be attacked and defeated by an
enemy. This is the military model. If you're fighting in a
battle, you avoid vulnerability. The problem is that this
model is entirely useless if you're striving for intimacy.
Many of us have been programmed since our early days on
the playground to avoid vulnerability so we wouldn't get
attacked by other kids. The choice is clear. Do we want to
avoid vulnerability with our beloved, or do we want to feel
the heights of love?

To be vulnerable, contrary to what many people think,
makes you truly attractive, even irresistible. The opposite
of vulnerability is keeping on your armor, your protection
from being hurt. Trouble is, this armor also keeps love
away from you.

To ask a woman for help with your fears, worries,
doubts or pain is to enlarge your trust of her, and thus to
really love her. To deeply receive a woman's love is to give
her the greatest gift.

Timing is important as well. You need to be sensitive to her level of receptivity. She may not be ready to drop everything just because you want to express your vulnerability. It may not work to blurt out your vulnerability as she races around the house after the children. It never hurts to ask her first: "Honey, I have something vulnerable to share with you. Is this a good time for you?" Then listen to see if she's really ready, not just automatically saying yes.

The First Time I was Vulnerable with Joyce

I can't emphasize enough how happy it makes Joyce when I vulnerably come to her for help. We both remember clearly the first time I showed my full vulnerability to her. It was when I was a first year medical student at Meharry Medical School in Nashville, Tennessee, a mostly African-American school and the only medical school to accept me. It was the fall of 1968, Martin Luther King had just been shot the previous April, and the whole country was in a state of unrest. I was naïve. I figured I could fit in and make friends. And I did make a few friends, but I also felt discriminated against. It was painful to walk into a classroom and be hit in the face by a wall of silence that may as well be made of brick.

In December, during the holiday break, I flew up to Buffalo, NY, to marry Joyce. We had a lovely, romantic, but way too short honeymoon, then packed up our car and drove down to Nashville. Nashville at that time was divided by one road into the "White" section and the "Black" section. We moved into an apartment on the white side of town (the only place that would rent to us).

On the morning I was to resume classes at Meharry, I was hit by a feeling of dread as I was saying goodbye to Joyce.

She looked into my eyes. "Barry, what's wrong?"

Joyce knows me sometimes better than I do. She can instantly tell when something's wrong.

I wanted to share with her how difficult it was to be discriminated against, but the only words that came out were, "It's hard to leave you."

In that moment, Joyce felt behind my words to my deepest vulnerability, my true need for her love and protection. She felt me entrusting my scared little boy-self into her care, even though I didn't have the courage at the time to actually speak those words.

When I finally got up my courage to leave our apartment on the white side of Nashville, and got into our car, I cranked down the window to see Joyce loving me more than ever. She seemed to be looking right through me and said, "Barry, I'm so in awe of your beauty."

It wasn't so much the words she spoke as it was the way she spoke them … and the way she was looking at me with so much love. She was seeing in that moment my highest self, the real me which I had not yet discovered. I didn't know what to do or how to receive this enormous gift of love. I lamely mumbled, "Gee, maybe you shouldn't be feeling that way." I'm not exactly proud of that comment. Thankfully, it didn't seem to faze Joyce.

All these years later, I realize my feeling of vulnerability was a great gift of love to Joyce. Showing her my fear and complete need for her love, empowered her to rise in love to see me in a deeper, more authentic way.

Joyce: Though Barry and I had been together for four years, he had never shown me his deepest vulnerability until that moment in Nashville right after our wedding and honeymoon. I had loved Barry from the beginning of our relationship but, through the vulnerability, I experienced a deeper part of him. It was as if the vulnerability had opened the door of his heart and allowed me to truly see him. I felt a power of love and compassion in Barry that I had never known before. I was only twenty-two at the time and did not have the experience or language to be able to express the emotion of love and adoration that I was feeling. That's why I said, "Barry, I'm so in awe of your beauty." He didn't understand my words and dismissed them, and that was all right with me. It was enough that I was feeling even deeper feelings of love for him.

The Power of Vulnerability

Recently we were doing a couple's retreat. We had the couples sit in a circle and each person, including Barry and me, took turns and spoke of their vulnerability. One man spoke of the vulnerability he was feeling because he had had an emotional affair with another woman over the course of several years. He had stopped having this emotional affair and had worked on the issue with his wife in counseling. But his wife felt unable to forgive or trust him and there was a distance between them. During the vulnerability process, this man shared about his emotional affair and the pain it had caused his wife. He said that he felt so bad about himself for causing a lack of trust in the relationship. His eyes filled with tears as he shared that he wondered if he could ever forgive himself.

As he was crying, his wife reached over, hugged him, and said, "I can finally forgive you. I needed to see your vulnerability and pain. Up until now it has only been me expressing the pain of what happened." At the end of the weekend, these two were much in love and told the group that they felt that now they could begin to develop a new relationship with each other built on honesty and vulnerability.

I remember a powerful time that Barry showed me his vulnerability. We were six months pregnant with our third child and went to the hospital on the advice of our midwife for an ultrasound. Our two little girls were with us. The doctor performing the ultrasound coldly told us that our baby was dead. I immediately became painfully vulnerable. Barry not only took care of me but also the details surrounding the operation to remove the body of the baby.

For months I felt like I was drowning in a vast sea of vulnerability, and the only productive thing I could do was to focus on caring for our two little girls. Barry was wonderful and took over my work and some of the household chores. But we began to drift apart emotionally.

One day, when our girls were with other people, Barry came into the room where I was trying to meditate. I looked up at him and saw his vulnerable expression as he said, "I'm just now feeling so sad that I lost a baby too."

I gratefully held him in my arms while he cried. His vulnerability that day was a great gift to me as it allowed me to come back into my power as I held him. Up until then, I felt lost in my need and grief. Barry's vulnerability was like a loving hand reaching into my strength and love, and tenderly bringing these qualities out. Until that moment, I was like a child needing Barry's fathering. His vulnerability brought out the loving mother in me, strengthening a part of me that had been badly shaken.

From that day on we felt such a united strength and healing in our common vulnerability which greatly helped not only our relationship, but our two little girls as well. I believe they needed to see their father's sadness and vulnerability.

> *I feel really loved by Bruce*
> *when he's willing to go to the scary inner places*
> *with me.*
> — Ruth Richardson, South Royalton, VT

Barry: It's often more difficult for men to show their vulnerability. We're so often raised with "machismo." We hear the messages, "Be a man. Men don't cry. Never show your fear." We're taught to hold in our feelings. We view all feelings except anger (and related feelings like frustration, irritation, and annoyance) as a sign of weakness. Yet it is our vulnerability that is our real strength, not the hollow bravado we usually display to the world.

After years of experience, Joyce and I have come to realize the extreme importance of vulnerability. I feel it is impossible to truly love another person without being vulnerable. I like the expression of "intimacy" as "into me see." To be intimate is to let your partner see into you ... all of you, not just the parts you like about yourself. Intimacy has come to mean sex for many people, but it is so much more. Vulnerability is the cornerstone of intimacy. Vulnerability allows you to be seen at the most fundamental level.

I love to lead men's retreats, and by the end of these weekends all the men understand the importance of vulnerability. During these weekends we experience the tenderness of fathering one another, and the liberation of having our inner little boys safely loved by other men as fathers. We share our pain, our fears, our shame, our feelings of unworthiness and insecurity. And most importantly, we experience how our vulnerability allows us to be more authentic, and how this authenticity makes us more loveable – and more powerful – in the eyes of every man present.

For most of the men, it's easier to be vulnerable at these weekend retreats with other men than it is to be vulnerable with the women in their lives. A standard of safety is established from the beginning of the retreat. They often admit that they lack this safety at home with their wives or partners. Some admit to being scared of women, that somehow women have the power to hurt them. Therefore, as a true solution to this problem, I challenge each man to bring their vulnerability to the important women in their lives. By doing this, they create the safety they need, rather than waiting for their women to create the safety for them. It's touching for me to hear from the wives and partners after a men's retreat. Quite often I am thanked by these women who are deeply moved by the vulnerability of their partners.

The Key to Vulnerability

So, aside from coming to one of my men's retreats, how can you show your vulnerability to the woman you love? How can you bless her with your vulnerability? The whole key is held by your inner little boy.

Yes, I had that extremely powerful moment of vulnerability with Joyce before returning to medical school in Nashville. But, I'm sorry to admit, I quickly buried that deep need for her love. I went back to life as usual, with my inner little boy closeted from view.

Three years later, then in my final year of medical school at the University of Southern California in Los Angeles, I was reading a new book, *Open Marriage*, and pressuring Joyce with my "need" for expanded sexual experiences. I remember one time in the living room of our tiny apartment in Highland Park, she tried to address the deeper issues. "Barry, I need your love. Don't you need mine?"

My vulnerability was too deeply hidden. "I love you, Joyce. I don't need you."

Then I went on to new heights of denial, "I can love other women fully, and it won't take anything away from our love. You're being selfish to want me all to yourself."

Joyce was in tears from the sheer arrogance of my words.

During this time of our lives in Los Angeles, we had a beloved teacher and friend, Leo Buscaglia. We knew him shortly before he became an American phenomenon, with many books on the New York Times bestseller list, and thousands of people lined up after his lectures to receive one of his famous hugs.

Leo loved Joyce!! He was her main preceptor in her master's program at the University of Southern California. And through Joyce, I had also felt close to Leo, although most of my time was occupied as a medical student at the same university.

He used to say to me, "Whatever Joyce feels is written all over her face. When she's sad, she cries. When she's happy, she smiles. When she's angry, it's visible. When she's at peace, her face is relaxed."

Then, with brutal honesty, he'd say to me, "I don't know what you're feeling. You can smile when you're angry or sad. So I can't trust your smile. Stop being phony, Barry!"

He was right, albeit blunt. I *was* hiding my sadness, anger, fear, and every other emotion I considered unpleasant. I had learned all my life, as many of us have, to cover up and ignore my vulnerability. A significant piece of this vulnerability was my human emotional need for Joyce – and for love in general.

To make matters worse, I crossed a sacred boundary and had sex with another woman. Joyce was devastated and left the marriage. She later sent me a note: "Barry, I will always love you. I understand that you need your freedom more than you need me. I now give you all the freedom in the world. You can do whatever you want. Please respect my decision to end our marriage. Don't try to contact me."

I thought I'd be happy with my newfound freedom but, after Joyce left, my life collapsed. I was alone – with my feelings. And up to the surface they came – agonizing pain, an aching hole of sadness in my heart. I was shocked and surprised by the intensity of these feelings.

After enduring the agony for a few days, I ignored Joyce's request and tried to find her. I called her friends, and they lovingly but firmly let me know that Joyce did not want to see me – ever!

Desperate, I knew I needed to ask Leo for help. Our apartment was a few houses down the street from his. I walked to his door and knocked. Leo opened the door a crack, saw that it was me, and quickly slid out onto the porch, closing the door behind him. I had no idea that Joyce was staying at his house, and she didn't want me to know where she was. As far as she was concerned, our relationship was over.

Leo looked at me inquisitively. Completely devoid of self-pride, I blurted out my despair, my face and tears finally matching my inner pain. Leo studied me until I finished blubbering. Then, to my utter surprise, a giant smile lit up his face and he grabbed me in one of his famous hugs. While squeezing me, he excitedly spoke, "Barry, you're finally real ... you're finally real!!"

Although I didn't share his rejoicing, I knew he was right. I was no longer hiding my vulnerability. And it did feel good to finally let my feelings out, and be comforted by another human being – and a very loving one.

That evening, for the first time in my life, I made peace with a little boy inside me that needed love, acceptance, and nurturing – the part of me that needed Joyce, needed God, needed everyone and everything. I made peace with my humanity, instead of pretending to be above it. I had been convinced that need and dependence, sadness and fear, and all so-called "negative" feelings, were signs of weakness. Now I realized the courage and strength it took to feel all my feelings – to be truly vulnerable. I had been convinced that feeling my humanity would prevent me from feeling my divinity. I now knew that feeling my divinity depended upon my feeling my humanity. We are human beings on a spiritual journey, and spiritual beings on a human journey.

After being with Leo, I had a bittersweet realization. I had lost my beloved wife, Joyce, and might carry remorse and regret for the remainder of my life. That was the bitter part. The sweet part was the gift of vulnerability, the gift of a fuller life, with all my feelings and, especially, the awareness of a little boy inside me who needs love.

Joyce: I stayed in our apartment the night that Barry told me of his affair. I had never experienced so much pain before, nor had I ever experienced so much anger for another human being. The day before I had sensed that Barry was sexually attracted to my girlfriend who was visiting from New York. I told him clearly that if he acted upon those feelings, I would not be able to handle it. The next day, while I was at work, he acted upon them anyway. I believe he never thought I would leave him. I was devoted to him. I had been supporting him through medical school, even though I was also in graduate school. I cooked every meal, cleaned, and tended to all of the household responsibilities. Medical school is an enormous amount of work and time. I tried to take care of everything so we could just enjoy each other when he had time off. We had a lot of fun and our sexual life together was thoroughly enjoyable for both of us.

The only really painful part of our relationship was when he told me he didn't need me and that he could love other women. It was at that point that we probably should have gone into counseling, but honestly being twenty-five and given the fact that it was the early seventies, I never even thought about it. I thought if I loved him enough, he would realize the special bond between us and realize he needed me just as much as I needed him. It was obvious to me that he needed me just as much, but painful that he could not see it. It was obvious to all of our friends and family as well.

To his credit, Barry told me about the affair with my friend as soon as he saw me. Although that honesty was important, he lacked any sense of remorse. In fact, he was proud of the fact that he had done it, proud that he had proved once and for all that he did not need me. He even said that this was the way he intended to live from now on. He wanted to stay married to me, but he also wanted the freedom to be with other women.

The word "NO" screamed out from a place deep within me. It was the biggest anger I had ever felt in my life. I knew without a doubt that I could not stay in the marriage one more moment. I felt like a thousand knives were piercing my heart at the same time.

After this explosion of feeling, I locked myself in our bathroom and remained there until I could get up quietly in the early morning dawn, pack a few things for myself, and take our dog. As I walked down the steps of our apartment, I also felt I was walking out of my marriage of three years. I would not answer any of his calls even when the secretary at my workplace begged me to talk to him so he would stop calling so often. I was done.

A week later, Barry got a note to me through a friend of mine. The note simply said, "Can I please just talk with you for fifteen minutes? I had a realization that has changed my life. I am so sorry for what I did."

Through my friend, a time was arranged. I entered the meeting with Barry with a totally closed heart and mind. My sense of betrayal was so huge that I was done with the relationship and nothing he could say could convince me otherwise. I was prepared to be strong and keep my boundaries. But I was not prepared for how he looked or for the message that he spoke.

Barry did not look good. Gone was the false pride and arrogance. He was pale and had obviously not been sleeping. He was completely vulnerable and it showed on his face. He spoke with authentic vulnerability, "Joyce, I know I've probably lost you forever because of the mistake I've made. I've finally realized my need for your love. If you could ever forgive me, I would like to start over. If not, I'll continue to live by myself and just feel this small child part of me that needs love."

I believe I said nothing. I stayed fifteen minutes and then walked out, just as I had planned to do. I was not ready to open up to him or give him any comfort whatsoever. He had hurt me in the worst possible way. And yet, for another week, I could think of nothing else but his vulnerability and his newfound feeling of needing my love. Even though I was angry and hurt, I was now also drawn to him.

I was at Leo's house for one of his famous "Love Classes." Leo knew exactly what was going on between Barry and me. At one point he spoke to the whole class while looking directly at me and said, "Everyone deserves a second chance."

I went into another room and called Barry. He walked the three minutes to Leo's house and brought me back to our apartment. Once inside, we fell into each other's arms and Barry kept saying, "I'm so sorry. I was such an arrogant fool. I now know how much I need your love."

We began the journey of healing. It took two years before I could fully trust him again. He stayed steadfast in his love for me and, especially, his need for my love. And, importantly, he believed in the change within himself and trusted that he would not make such a mistake again. Eventually, I began to believe that as well.

Had Barry not approached me with vulnerability, I don't believe we would have made it as a couple. The vulnerability was strong enough to draw me even though I was determined not to come back.

I feel such a deep sense of gratitude for the vulnerability that Barry was able to feel and show me. That was forty-two years ago. We have raised three children, written six books and led countless retreats. Barry has made the most wonderful partner I could ever imagine. He rarely misses the opportunity to tell me that he loves and needs me. I feel like the most blessed woman in the world. And to think that all these blessings nearly ended before they even began. Such is the power of vulnerability.

I love that Barry is strong and able to help people with his love and caring. I love that he is nurturing to me and our children. But I also love the part of Barry that needs me and is able to show me his vulnerable side. Every once in a while something will happen, like a painful memory from his childhood, or a negative experience. Then he comes to me and tells me that he needs me and asks me to hold him. I'm so thrilled to do this. I hold him, comfort him, and allow him to talk. Sometimes, during these times, he looks just like a little hurt boy. I love that he trusts me enough to see that part of him. It feels so good whenever he comes to me in this way. There are many different ways that he loves me, and this is definitely one of them.

You become more attractive to a woman when your strength is balanced by your vulnerable need for her love. This expression of need is different from the need for sex, which is good, but different. Of course, your expression of need must be balanced with your acceptance of the woman's need for you as well. If the expression of your need is more than the expression of her need, then this will not be attractive to her. Also the timing of the expression is important.

But given that the time is appropriate and that he also nurtures her and holds her in her vulnerable times, then his expression of need can be beautiful, fulfilling and empowering for a woman. It can be a gift, another way of truly loving her and honoring her wisdom and compassion.

Barry: If you, like a lot of men, ignore this little child part of you, you cannot be vulnerable. Yes, you love a woman by being powerful, by protecting her from all harm, by fathering the little girl inside her, and by gently taking the lead. But without vulnerability your loving is incomplete.

Some ways to be more vulnerable with a woman:

Ask her for help. If you don't ask her for help, you foster the illusion that you don't need her. But you do need her … in a thousand ways. And don't only ask for help in physical ways, like helping you hang a picture. Ask for emotional support, like holding you when you feel sad, or for reassurance when you feel insecure. Ask for spiritual help too, like sitting with you in prayer or meditation.

Admit that you need her love. When a woman feels needed *as well as* protected, she feels really loved. If she feels needed but not protected, then she goes into "mother mode," and you become another one of her children. Definitely not attractive to her! When she feels you need her love as much as she needs yours, she can relax into the relationship.

Be courageous enough to admit your fears to her. Yes, you have just as many fears as she does. Women tend to speak more about their fears. You may hold them inside, or worse, not even be aware of them. That does not mean you're less afraid. Admit your fears about money, not being good enough, or even losing her through death. This makes you more human, more vulnerable, and definitely more attractive to her.

Let her know, without anger, when you feel hurt by her. It's easy to bypass hurt feelings and jump right into anger. Even though I more typically express my anger, reflexively covering over my hurt, I sometimes will let Joyce know I feel hurt by something she did or said. Showing my hurt, without the anger, shows Joyce my vulnerability. It also shows her how important she is to me. She loves this and will usually immediately apologize.

> *I feel Simon's love most deeply when he reveals to me his most vulnerable inner landscape. When he allows himself to be young in my presence and small in my arms. When he asks me "do you love me?" even though he knows without a doubt that the answer is a resounding yes...he asks nonetheless because there is a small, sweet part of him that longs to hear it, to be reassured, to be held by my love. When he can allow himself to ask....he is trusting me with the bigness of his own love.*
> *–Tamra Rutherford*

When I Most Needed Joyce

Sometimes vulnerability can be extreme. The following story tells about a time when I needed Joyce more than any other time in my life.

It was Saturday, June 20, 2009. I had no idea that this day would shake my whole world – and that my very life would depend upon Joyce.

The new refrigerator I ordered arrived and I emptied out all the food from the old one. I found a frozen piece of chocolate cake baked by our son months before and couldn't resist tasting it. It was still delicious!

After the new refrigerator was filled and shelves adjusted, I made myself a cup of green tea, went into the office, and started working on the computer. I had only been in the office for about ten minutes and had a few sips of the tea, when I started feeling light-headed with a strange "buzzing" in my head. At first, I thought I was hypoglycemic, or maybe the green tea somehow had an unusually large amount of caffeine by accident. But the sensation felt different from anything I had ever experienced. It was not at all unpleasant, just unusual. And it was getting stronger by the minute! The "buzzing" was now spreading throughout my whole body.

I got down on my hands and knees, touching my forehead to the office carpet, hoping to bring more blood to my brain. It didn't help. It kept getting stronger. I thought, "Maybe I'm down on my hands and knees to pray for help, or to be closer to the earth." I did indeed pray for help.

VISSELL

Sitting on my chair again, ever the medical doctor, I wondered if I was having a stroke. Not your typical stroke that involves sensory loss or paralysis, but an atypical one that was heightening my sensations. I even thought about Jill Bolte Taylor's description of her own stroke in her book, *My Stroke of Insight: A Brain Scientist's Personal Journey.*

There was only one thing in the whole world I wanted to do – and that was to find Joyce. I got up off the floor, not at all sure I could stand, let alone walk. I found I needed to will myself to put one foot in front of the other, that walking didn't seem to come naturally, but my balance seemed okay. I made it to the kitchen, found Joyce, and let her know I needed her help. It has often been difficult for me to ask Joyce for help, to lean on her strength and love, but in this moment it was a "no-brainer."

She took one look into my eyes and immediately knew something was very wrong. Although my pupils seemed normal, my eye movements were sluggish and my skin was cold and clammy. She helped me lie down on the couch, sitting close to me, and together we tried to piece together what was going on. My thinking faculties seemed fine, even hyper-alert. Caffeine overdose was out of the question. It was only green tea, which has little caffeine. Stroke seemed unlikely, too.

Now, my skin was becoming hypersensitive. The blanket Joyce had placed upon me felt like it was filled with lead. Even her hands upon me felt oppressively heavy … a clear warning sign. Normally, there's nothing I like more than Joyce's touch.

I kept returning in my mind to the chocolate cake. Poisoning was growing higher on the list of possibilities. But really ... chocolate cake? In the freezer? Then Joyce and I wondered if John-Nuri had added something "special" to the recipe ... something that could be mind-altering. Our twenty-year-old son was at a party with his friends, and Joyce called his cell phone and left an urgent message.

Even though it had been more than 35 years since our "experimenting" with psychedelics, I knew I was not experiencing a "bad trip." There was no mind altering, no euphoria, or distorted perceptions ... just this intense physical sensation that was vibrating or buzzing without pain. And just when I would think it couldn't get any stronger, it got worse!

Joyce was on the phone, trying to reach a doctor friend. On the couch, I had the oddest sensation of starting to go to sleep without being even remotely sleepy. It felt like my body was shutting down internally and I, my real self, my conscious self, was somehow detaching from my body. I was starting to feel profoundly peaceful, more peaceful than I have ever felt. Letting go in that moment would have been blissfully easy, but another part of me understood that this could very well be my body's way of dying. I somehow intuitively felt that, as intense as the poison was, I had a choice of whether to stay or leave. I even thought about Rami and River's wedding in exactly one week. I needed to be there! Rami needed me to be there to bless her union with River. And I had so much more to give and experience in my own life.

I called out, "JOYCE, I REALLY NEED YOU!!!" I felt in that moment that I needed her more than any other time in my life.

She heard the vulnerability in my voice and rushed over to sit close to me.

I locked onto her eyes as if they were a lifeline and asked, "Please keep looking into my eyes! Keep me engaged! Help me stay awake! Please help anchor me to my body!"

"Barry, I'm scared. Should I call 911 and get you to the emergency room?"

Somehow, it just didn't feel right. Even though I was now convinced that my body was processing some kind of poison, I felt I was at the peak of its toxic effects. The next few minutes seemed critical. I didn't want to spend those few precious minutes in the company of paramedics and emergency medical protocols.

Perhaps I was being naïve, perhaps I was in denial, but I really wanted to stay at home, surrounded by love and quiet. Some moments, I wondered if I was dying, so intense was the experience. Other moments, I felt I had the conscious decision to live or die.

I felt extremely vulnerable. I also felt more need for Joyce's loving energy than I had ever felt in my life.

"No," I finally managed to answer. "Just stay with me and help me stay in my body. I just can't do this by myself."

In that moment, she felt like my lifeline ... physically, emotionally and spiritually.

Joyce went into prayer with her eyes open and focused more than I have ever seen her. There was a living stream of love pouring from her eyes into my eyes … into my body. I felt more held in that moment than I have ever felt. I was being spiritually, emotionally and physically held by just her eyes.

Several times, her eyes and face started to go out of focus, and I felt myself slipping away. Joyce seemed to sense this, and would speak to me in a soothing but firm voice that would bring me back into my body.

What felt like a lifetime was only a matter of minutes. My body started to shake and Joyce found more blankets to put on me. I couldn't tell if I was cold or hot. I just wasn't that connected to my body.

John-Nuri arrived home and breathlessly entered the room. He assured us there was nothing unusual in the cake, and I knew he was speaking the truth.

It was then that I finally remembered something else I had tasted during my busyness in the kitchen. It was my homegrown kombucha. Widely revered for its immune strengthening properties, it looks like a mushroom but is really a symbiotic relationship between bacteria and yeast that is grown in a solution of sugar and black tea. The preparation had been growing for several months, and I remembered sampling the solution about an hour before my symptoms started. It tasted normal. Luckily, I only poured myself about two ounces of the drink. Had I poured myself a full glass, you would probably not be reading these words right now.

My medical friend later told me, after much research and several calls to Poison Control, that my kombucha culture had somehow become contaminated. Some stray organism invaded the mixture, reproduced itself, and secreted a neurotoxin that poisoned me. There have been other cases of poisoning with homegrown kombucha, including one reported death.

The strange buzzing was beginning to subside. I gradually recovered from my ordeal.

I feel so different as a result of this near death experience. I have never felt so grateful to be alive. I notice I take more time to give and receive love with friends and family. Having been so close to death really forces me to appreciate life, to slow down and notice all the beauty around me, to be a better and more vulnerable human being.

I am so aware of the fragility of our bodies. Two ounces of a drink placed me on the brink of a precipice. A fraction of a second is all that is needed to destroy a human body in a car accident. How much have I taken life for granted. I realize that every minute of life is precious. Every day holds the opportunity for more growth and love.

I give thanks for the gift of vulnerability, that my need for Joyce's love allows me to feel like a stronger and better man. My vulnerability also allows me to better understand and provide a safe container for Joyce's vulnerability.

"…Let me drown in your laughter.
Let me die in your arms.
Let me lay down beside you.
Let me always be with you…"
– "Annie's Song" by John Denver

To Really Trust a Woman

TO REALLY LOVE A WOMAN IS TO GIVE HER YOUR COMPLETE TRUST. I love the line in Bryan Adams's song, "… and when you find yourself lying helpless in her arms, you know you really love a woman." To lie helpless in her arms, you need to give up control and be vulnerable. You need to trust that she will not intentionally hurt you, that she is looking out for your well-being, fully on your side, and watching your back. Even more importantly, you can trust in a higher power expressing through your beloved, an abundance of love and caring that can come through her.

In fact, so much of this book is about learning how to really trust her in every area of your relationship. Becoming vulnerable with a woman teaches you all about trust. I often hear, "I'll be more vulnerable with her when I trust her more." This attitude doesn't work. Your vulnerability opens the door to trust, and trust opens the door to love. "Lying helpless in her arms" proves that you can trust her.

Ask Her For Help

My father, although often a loving man, was prone to noisy outbursts of anger. As a child, these "temper tantrums" affected me deeply. To cope, I learned to tune out the abrasive yelling, to not even hear it on a conscious level. It was my way of protecting my sensitive feelings.

This coping skill got me through my childhood, but no longer served me as an adult. In my relationship with Joyce, if something I did upset her and she expressed her feelings to me, my lifelong skill of tuning out and thus not hearing her was anything but helpful. It only provoked her into more upset and anger. So, with Joyce as my teacher, I have been learning to overcome my fear of strong emotions, and to healthily express my own anger.

But I didn't stop there. I knew it was even more important to practice showing my hurt, the vulnerable feeling that often precedes anger by mere milliseconds. As I started showing my hurt to Joyce, the safest person in the world for me, I realized my next step was to show this to my own dad. So, in the early autumn of 1994, with my parents' annual Thanksgiving visit approaching in November, I asked Joyce for help. I entered training with Joyce as my "feelings coach." I asked her to help me stay in my body and feelings if my dad erupted, rather than disappear or go numb.

Joyce assured me with absolute certainty that, at some point in the visit, my dad would inevitably explode into some degree of a temper tantrum. I committed myself to be prepared to vulnerably express my hurt. I had learned to confront him with my anger, but this was not my highest truth. It was still a cover-up, keeping me protected. Shortly before the Thanksgiving visit, I finally felt ready. I trusted Joyce to be able to help me in this blind spot with my dad.

When my parents arrived, I felt a little bit awkward trying to be relaxed and enjoy the visit while at the same time staying vigilant. A day went by without a blow-up, then another, and I wondered if I would have an opportunity to put my training into practice. Joyce coached me to be patient, but to stay ready.

On the third day, my dad and I were in the kitchen preparing a meal. Joyce and my mom were visiting nearby at the table. I noticed my father was starting to get stressed about not finding the right ingredients for a dish he was preparing. The tension was building like the pressure of magma in the core of an ancient volcano. Joyce gave me her best supportive coach's look of encouragement. She knew in that moment what was coming.

My father finally blew. He started yelling at my mother, even though she was sitting at our table and had nothing to do with the missing ingredients. My stomach tightened in the all-too-familiar fear of my childhood. But instead of tuning out to avoid my feelings, I remembered all of Joyce's help. I noticed and felt how much my dad's yelling was actually painful to me.

I knew my time had arrived and I had to seize the moment. I ran across the kitchen and stopped two feet in front of my dad. I reached out and lovingly but firmly took his shoulders in my hands, looked into his eyes, and said without anger, "Dad, your yelling is hurting me very much."

I will never forget the look of utter surprise in my dad's face. This was a completely new experience for him. His emotional outbursts were so automatic to him that he didn't even realize they had an effect upon anyone else. To my astonishment, his face softened and he replied, "Barry, the last thing I ever want to do is hurt you."

Soon there were tears in both of our eyes, and we hugged each other close. In that moment, I felt closer to my dad than I had in a long time. I also felt victorious. I had been able to express my hurt without anger or blame. I was finally being functional in a situation where I previously had only been dysfunctional.

I expected that I would need to vulnerably confront my father several times during the visit. But I never had to do it again. It was a great visit after that confrontation. Yes, I had to be vulnerably honest with my father in subsequent visits, but it became easier and easier.

Then, a year and a half later, my dad died suddenly. What comforted me most in my grieving was that experience of being vulnerable with my father. I am so grateful for the opportunity to break out of an unconscious pattern from childhood. Asking for Joyce's help allowed me to trust her so much more.

When I didn't Trust Joyce.

When we used to have heated arguments in our late teens and early twenties, it sometimes felt like she was out to get me, that we were on different sides, even that our relationship was threatened. We still get angry, even heatedly so, but now I trust Joyce. I trust that no matter how angry she is at me, she is still committed to getting back to loving me. This is no little thing. I trust that she will do whatever it takes to open her heart to me, and this helps me to be more accountable for my own anger. It gives me permission to find ways to open my heart to her as well.

I used to have difficulty trusting Joyce while co-leading groups. When we were both twenty-seven, she joined me in doing group process work. I had more training and experience. I "knew" more than she did, and she thought so as well. She often meekly sat beside me, while I did most of the leading. Then she realized it didn't matter that I *knew* more. She started listening to her intuition, and loving each person completely. I may have been the therapist, but she was the lover. It didn't take me long to see the light. When group participants felt loved by Joyce, they felt safer and opened up more. I started to see the wisdom of the goddess coming through her. I learned to trust that wisdom, to depend on it.

However, old habits die slowly. Perhaps our greatest challenge in working together has been my old habit of being the therapist, of interrupting Joyce to make a point. Coming more from the heart, Joyce is quieter and slower to speak, with sometimes-long pauses between her words. Additionally, she grew up in a family where people actually listened to one another, where one person stopped talking and then another began. I, on the other hand, grew up in a family where everyone talked at the same time, and whoever talked louder might be the one heard. There was no such thing as a pause between words, let alone sentences. Even the slightest pause was simply an invitation for someone to butt in.

So Joyce would be speaking to the group, and there would be a pause while she searched deeply for the right words. I would feel uncomfortable with this thing called silence between words, a gap that must be filled with sound, and would jump in to save the day. This would, of course, hurt Joyce. To her it was an act of disrespect. She felt not trusted, not needed, even not wanted. At times she has even considered giving up working together with me leading groups.

I love Joyce by trusting her completely in front of a group. I love her by creating room for her to share her wisdom, by making space for the goddess, by sitting back and drinking in her love-infused words. I love her by trusting that she can say things I can't, that her perspective balances mine, that the two of us united are much more effective than either one of us as individuals.

Sometimes Joyce Perceives Things that I don't.

In one of our early groups, there was a single woman who needed my love in a way that crossed over a subtle line, but a line that Joyce saw and felt. In just one moment, while saying goodbye to her, with just a few words, I allowed myself to be the one to fill her need. Energetically, I crossed that same subtle line from professional to personal. Joyce whispered, "Now you're in trouble, Barry. Just wait and see."

I looked at her incredulous. "What are you talking about?"

"You gave something to her that wasn't yours to give. Just watch. Now she'll want a whole lot more."

Joyce was right. This woman started stalking me, and it required significant time and energy to stop her.

I trust Joyce has much to teach me in so many areas. I trust her instincts. I listen when she gets an inner yes or no. I trust her sensitivity. I trust she feels things that I haven't learned to feel yet. I trust her wisdom. She has a way of seeing things in a way I don't. She has a perspective that I don't have.

Most of all, I trust her love for me. It is unfailing. Even when she's mad at me, she still loves me.

And she often tells me how good it feels that I trust her
so deeply.

Trust Practice

> Write down at least 10 ways you
> trust your woman. It may surprise you
> how many ways you do trust her.
> Show her the list, or even better, tell
> her in your own words.

Taking Care of the Relationship as Much as She Does

🧍

Initiate quality time together.

JOYCE AND I HAVE SEEN SO MANY COUPLES WHERE IT FALLS TO THE WOMAN TO TAKE CARE OF THE RELATIONSHIP. If she wants special time with her mate, she is the one who needs to make all the arrangements. We're looking forward to the day when we start a couple's workshop and find out more than half the couples are there because of the man's initiative. Sadly, it's usually the woman who brings (and occasionally drags) her man to our programs. When the woman is the one taking care of the relationship, she ends up feeling like he just doesn't care. If the work on the relationship is not equally shared by both partners, then the love cannot be fully shared either.

Often, the man is the initiator during the courting phase of the relationship – no matter how busy he is. He may be more motivated because he is less secure about the relationship. He may be still trying to win her affection. Then, over time, he may grow comfortable and secure that she loves him, is fully committed, and will always be there. Therefore he may stop initiating opportunities to deepen the love. When this becomes intolerable for the woman, because she no longer feels important to him, she'll want to leave the relationship. She may then announce her intentions, and this mobilizes the man into action, because he now feels insecure. Sadly, not long after he sees that she is once again committed to him, he slips back into his world of complacency. We see this hopeless cycle time after time.

Alternatively, you find yourself initiating special time with her with the hope that it will lead to sex. You set up romantic evenings. You light candles and put on her favorite music but, if sex doesn't happen, you feel disappointed. The whole evening then feels like a set-up to her. She doesn't really feel loved. She needs to know that she is more important than sex, that you are excited just to be with her, to talk with her, to look into her eyes.

I admit, there were times earlier in our relationship when I was guilty of allowing sex to become more important than Joyce, and then felt disappointed when she wasn't in the mood. How could she be in the mood for sex when she wasn't feeling more important than my desires?

I am learning that sex is not the only way to unite with Joyce. I love her best when I invite her to share spiritual time with me. We have established spiritual rituals, such as beginning the day with a spoken prayer, or sharing a morning meditation together, or a prayer before we eat. Joyce particularly loves it when I spontaneously initiate spiritual moments, like taking her hands in the middle of the day, touching foreheads together and speaking a prayer. She loves it when I ask her to sit with me for a meditation ... anytime!

Don't get me wrong, Joyce is a powerful leader in our relationship. She has no trouble initiating activities that replenish our love, but she loves it when I take charge. As long as we both take just as much initiative in caring for our relationship, we remain in balance.

One evening a few years ago, my husband Steve came in while I was washing my face. He said, "let me show you something," and held out his hand for the washcloth. He rinsed it in hot running water, then instructed me to close my eyes, lean my head back and breathe through my mouth. He laid the warm wet cloth on my face, carefully arranging the corners so that my throat and forehead were fully covered. It felt good but I complained that my ears were cold. Immediately, he placed his two warm hands over my ears, and I felt like I was in heaven. It was not so much the washcloth that warmed me, as Steve's gentle spontaneous act of caring. I basked in a spiritual glow, feeling totally surrounded and blessed by his love. Steve died last year, and I cherish this memory.
–Paulianne Balch-Rancourt, Port Orford, OR

Taking initiative is different from taking control.

Taking initiative is honoring her feelings and the relationship. Taking control is honoring mainly your own feelings or needs.

There is only one situation where Joyce wants me to take control, and that's in our canoe. This is especially the case when we are paddling into rapids on a river. Even though I welcome her to take control with me, she has no interest in learning river running skills. She's there to enjoy nature, something we both equally enjoy. She wants me to take complete charge in rapids and issue commands to her. We laugh about this. It's the only time in our relationship when I have full permission to order her around – even forcefully. She sits in the bow (front of the canoe) and awaits my commands. Sometimes I yell "forward paddle," sometimes "back paddle," and sometimes "down," when we're about to hit a wave or hole. She immediately slides backwards off her seat and lies down in the boat, effectively stabilizing the canoe by lowering her center of gravity, and moving her weight backwards to allow the bow to ride higher and keep us from swamping (filling with water). I suppose I could feel like a dog trainer at that moment, but I would never abuse the authority Joyce gives me.

Other than that specialized situation, Joyce and I take equal initiative in our relationship. In other words, our relationship holds just as high a priority for both of us.

Joyce: Spirituality is very important to me. When I have time alone, I want to meditate or read my spiritual books. It is really more important to me than anything else in life. Spending time in a spiritual way is also important to Barry, though not as much as to me. I love it when Barry agrees to spend time with me in a spiritual way or, even better, initiates this himself. This is perhaps the greatest way that Barry shows his love to me, and helps to take care of our relationship.

There are many things that are important in a healthy couple relationship: communication, healing the past, respect, appreciation, gratitude, sexuality, cooperation, compromise, having fun together, and the list goes on. But the most important is allowing for spiritual time when two people can connect soul-to-soul and heart-to-heart. This type of connection is the deepest and most fulfilling for two people, for it allows the inner spiritual being to be felt by the other. By "spiritual" we don't necessarily mean "religious," but rather a conscious recognition of something (an energy or love) bigger than your bodies, egos, and personalities.

The 10-Minute Challenge

In our couples' retreats, Barry and I challenge each couple to devote ten minutes a day to connecting spiritually. Usually, when we bring this up, there are groans and complaints from at least half the people:

"We don't have enough time to do this."

"If you saw our schedules you would know why this is impossible."

"We could maybe find time once a week for ten minutes, but every day would be out of the question."

We then go on to point out that many people spend at least one hour in front of the TV each day, perhaps fifteen minutes a day reading the newspaper, maybe half an hour of extraneous computer time, including Facebook or other social media, probably too long on the toilet reading, and other unnecessary uses of time. Usually the complaints stop at this point, and the couples begin to evaluate how they can salvage ten minutes a day for connecting spiritually.

We once heard about a famous yoga teacher who told his students, "If you spend ten minutes a day practicing yoga, it will change your life." Barry and I had always assumed that at least an hour of yoga a day was the minimum. Now we feel differently about the ten minutes of yoga we do on busy days.

The same is true for spiritual connection with couples. Ten minutes a day will change your lives and relationship.

Here are some suggestions for the ten minutes together:

Barry and I like to sit together quietly either in our living room or at a place outdoors, depending on the weather. We close our eyes and feel our love. We meditate silently for a while. We each speak a prayer of thanksgiving for our relationship, followed by a prayer asking for help. Then we like to look into each other's eyes and feel the deeper connection of our souls. On busy days we just take ten minutes. On less busy days we take longer.

Another wonderful thing to do is to listen to a favorite song while you are looking into each other's eyes.

Some couples like to use the ten minutes to deeply appreciate each other.

Other couples like to light a candle and read something from a spiritual book.

Some couples like to look into each other's eyes in silence while in a beautiful place.

These are just a few suggestions. The important thing is that the couples connect soul-to-soul and allow a higher power to bless their relationship. The ten minutes a day spent in such a nurturing spiritual way could save hours of arguing and unhappy feelings with one another. Feeling the depth of your partner's soul allows for deeper understanding, love and harmony.

This ten-minute plan only works if you both share the lead. Take turns suggesting a spiritual practice for the day, or initiating your time together. If spirituality is more important to her, she will naturally take the lead in this area but, in the end, she will not necessarily feel loved by you as a passive participant. Love her by initiating a form of spirituality that speaks to your heart as well.

One couple's response to the 10-Minute Challenge

Usually, in every couple's retreat, we have one or two couples who take us up on this ten-minute challenge. The couples who do are the ones who consistently report back to us about the deeper connection they are enjoying. The following is a letter from one such couple:

Dear Joyce and Barry,

We tremendously enjoyed your couple's retreat and decided that we would devote ten minutes a day to connecting spiritually. It was Jim's idea that we wake up ten minutes earlier. At first this seemed difficult, as we already get up early, but we persisted. After we dress, we take our coffee and sit together in the living room. (Our children are still sleeping.) Each day we take turns choosing a special song that would open our hearts to one another. As the song softly plays, we look into one another's eyes. When the song ends we close our eyes and each of us says a prayer for our relationship. Then we appreciate one another. We always end with a long hug and kiss. Jim then grabs some breakfast and is out the door for his commute to work. Soon the children wander down the stairs and I am off and running for another busy day.

Before we started this ten minutes of connection, Jim would be gone while I was still getting out of bed. I wouldn't hear from him until he came home at night and, when he walked in the door, there was often tension between us. After we started our "ten-minute plan," Jim would call me several times from work just to say he loved me. I found myself eagerly waiting for him to come home from work. Connecting in a deeper way seemed to last all day and give us an uplifting, close feeling. I realize now that the ten minutes of spiritual connection has become the most important part of our day. Thank you Joyce and Barry.

Love, Lisa.

If people only knew how this daily spiritual connection could enhance their relationship, they would never hesitate to make the commitment. Taking this time to connect spiritually is the most important use of ten minutes. It is worth any sacrifice, even if that means waking up ten minutes early. If you are in a relationship, I would like to challenge you to make this commitment. If you do, you will be amazed at how much closer you feel to one another.

The Gift of Positivity

A BEAUTIFUL WAY TO LOVE YOUR WOMAN IS TO KEEP YOUR THOUGHTS POSITIVE. This is not always possible. However, offering positive, grateful thoughts and words will strongly bless your relationship.

Some examples of "negative" husbands

I know a woman from another country whose husband had to retire early from his stressful job because of a medical condition. The doctor strongly recommended a peaceful life with no stress, perhaps developing a new hobby. He did start gardening and walking, which helped him tremendously. But he also started spending large amounts of time on the internet reading about problems in his country's government. Each morning he would rise early and read eight different newspapers looking for more information. Then he went on blog sites and every other kind of site he could find. The information he found made him angry and frustrated. Because he had few friends, his wife was the main person he could talk to about this. She told me that she sometimes did not want to go home after her workday because he would want to tell her everything he had found out that day. It was all negative and depressing to her and she was not interested. Day after day, she had to listen to this unpleasant news.

When she told him she wasn't interested, he got hurt and told her how important it was to him that she listen. This became quite a big problem in their relationship and served to create distance between them. If she didn't listen, he was hurt. If she did, she felt depressed by his negativity. She also worried about the effect of all of this bad news upon his health. She longed to have normal conversations that inspired and uplifted both of them. She also longed to tell him the positive things that had happened in her day. When she tried to do so, he seemed not to listen, and eventually related it all back to the negative condition in their country.

I know another woman whose husband worked full time. She stayed at home and tried to make their home a peaceful, sacred place. She cooked delicious meals for her husband and kept the home clean and orderly. Meanwhile her husband was obsessed with news of war. He had been in the Vietnam War and focused all of his energy on reading everything he could about any war that was going on in the world. Sometimes he got so angry at what he learned that he would yell at her. This woman longed for peaceful conversations. She understood that learning about war, wherever it was, was important to her husband. But did it have to be all of the time? Couldn't there also be some peace and focus on positive situations? She even bought a subscription to a newspaper that focused on positive news in the world. Her husband refused to read it or to even listen when she wanted to talk about it. As you can imagine, this woman was unhappy in her relationship. And so was the husband.

Another husband was just plain negative. If his wife liked a certain movie they had gone to, he would complain about the boring parts. If she was talking about one of her friends, he would point out something that he didn't like about that person. If their child received a B on a very difficult test, he complained that he should have gotten an A. If his wife lost ten pounds and was proud of it, he pointed out that she needed to lose another thirty. You can just imagine that this man's wife eventually stopped sharing with her husband.

Another example is the raging driver. This type of husband can be actually quite sweet and content while at home. But get him behind the wheel of a car and a different personality emerges altogether. He yells at every other driver that he perceives makes a mistake. He notices every fault and yells obscenities. The main trouble here is that none of these drivers can hear him or care what he is saying. The only person who can hear him is his wife sitting right next to him. Going on a date to the movies and dinner, or even driving to church can turn into a nightmare within the car with all of the yelling and accusing. Women have told me they would rather just stay at home and not go anywhere with their partner who drives like this.

And finally there is the chronic reporter of physical ailments. Some people feel they must tell their mates every detail of the pain in their body, even if they have had this situation for a long time and are not doing anything about it. Yes it is good to report conditions in the body, but if that is all you are talking about, it can get tiring and even boring.

Barry's Gift of Positivity to Me

Sometimes I take Barry's positivity for granted until I talk with other women. Then I realize how much his focus on the positive has helped our relationship. I like to talk about things for which I am grateful and, at dinner, Barry will join right in. Sometimes we will talk for the entire meal about things that make us happy.

Because of our work, we hear about others' pain and hardships. We feel a dedication and passion for helping people in their most difficult times. Because of this, we have vowed to bring positivity into our lives and not dwell on the sadness in the world. I believe this attitude has helped us in our work with people and certainly in our relationship.

Of course, this is not always possible. We, along with everyone else, have our share of challenges and hardships but, even in the hardest times, we try to help each other to feel grateful.

This gift of positivity can help your relationship with your woman tremendously. I would rather have Barry's positive thoughts and words than the gift of flowers. I truly love flowers and am absolutely thrilled whenever he brings them home to me, but the positive, grateful thoughts and words are like a fragrance that bathes my heart in such a beautiful way and lingers long after the flowers would have died.

Last year, when Barry had knee replacement surgery, he was in a lot of pain. I was busy helping him, keeping his ice machine full of ice, bringing him drinks, food and medicine. I could tell by his face that there was a lot of pain, and he was honest with me when I questioned him. However, he mostly appreciated me for all I was doing for him. He kept a positive attitude, even through his pain and sadness not to be able to go outside and do the things that he loved doing. His positive attitude was a definite gift to me in a challenging time in his life. He made me feel appreciated, needed and important.

You Love Her by Taking Care of Yourself

YOU REALLY LOVE A WOMAN WHEN YOU TAKE CARE OF YOUR BODY AND YOUR SOUL. This may seem obvious, but to many men it isn't. You may feel you take care of her, but if you don't take care of yourself, how can you really take care of her? I love the analogy of the flight attendant instructing passengers to put their own oxygen mask on first and then help their children or others put on their masks. There's often a parent who doesn't understand this, and wants to put their child's mask on first. But how much can you offer your child if you pass out from lack of oxygen?

The same applies to your relationship. If you don't breathe in the divine oxygen, how much can you really give to her? If you don't take care of your body, she will live in fear of your body breaking down. If you don't exercise or eat a healthy diet, you may be triggering her fear of abandonment. This is not really caring for her or yourself. If you don't take quiet time to nourish your soul, you can't really nourish her soul. Ultimately, if you don't take the time to love yourself, you will be running on empty, and she will not feel loved. She may feel needed, but not loved.

She may feel you receiving from her, but not giving to her. She may feel provided for financially, but not emotionally or spiritually.

Joyce's Greatest Fear

She is not afraid of dying before me. Her fear is of being left in this life without her "best friend." It's actually quite an honor for me. I feel so important to her. I feel the same way. I have the same fear of being left alone here on earth, but my taking good physical, psychological, emotional and spiritual care of myself is one way I can comfort her fear.

Joyce understands my need for outdoor adventures. Even though I take far fewer physical risks than I used to, I understand that any risk I take may trigger her fear of losing me. It doesn't work for me to stop taking all risks. To do that I would need to stop driving a car. Instead, I keep reassuring Joyce with my commitment to avoid any unnecessary risks. For example, on my solo river trips, I take the most conservative routes through all the rapids. I avoid the big holes, and the big thrills that go along with them, because of the risk of flipping the raft and potentially putting me in danger. On my canoe trips I'm even more conservative, lining my canoe around even small class II rapids. Joyce feels loved by this.

Joyce feels loved by all the things I do to take care of my body. She wants me to stay here on this earth for as long as she does. She knows the statistics: women live longer than men. She doesn't want us to follow this statistic.

The other way I comfort her is to reassure her that, if it does happen that I die before her, I will stay close to her as long as she needs me. I will bless her and love her. I will protect her from harm as much as I am able with invisible arms of light. I will do my utmost to communicate my love and the wisdom of the higher realms. As long as she wants me close, she will never be alone in this world.

> *Molly, it's amazing. The love … you get to take it with you (after you die).*
> – Sam, from the movie, Ghost.

"I'll be back in thirty minutes."

Joyce: It was a warm, windy and gorgeous afternoon in Hawaii. We had just brought our couples group to snorkel at the Kapoho Tide Pools, in the southeastern part of the Big Island of Hawaii. Where we enter the water, there's a large protected tide pool where I like to swim. Then there's a narrow channel with often fast-moving current that connects the tide pool with other less protected tide pools closer to the breaking waves. This is where Barry likes to go. What is the draw for him? This is where more of the turtles spend their time. These giant sea turtles are a joy to see. They are so graceful they look like angels gliding through the water. I love to see the turtles, but am a little scared of what it takes to get to them. We do not recommend this more risky snorkeling unless a person has a lot of experience. Most people in our group stay with me where the snorkeling is still nice, or venture out into the ocean a little bit.

As is our tradition, he swims over to me before he leaves, gives me a kiss and then says, "I'll be back in thirty minutes." I check my watch and Barry starts his stopwatch. Barry gives me a definite time when he will be back, and then he makes sure that he is back by that time or even a little early. This is a way he loves me, as I tend to worry about him when he goes so far away that I can't see him.

Barry: Thirty minutes is plenty of time for this particular adventure. Even so, I constantly monitor the time and frequently arrive back with Joyce about five minutes early. She is always happy (and relieved) to see me. During the time I am away from her, she tries hard not to worry about me. She prays for my safety. If I wait till the last minute to return, it's harder on Joyce. I know that the last five minutes are the hardest for her. And forget it if I lose track of the time and come back late. That's torture for my beloved.

Keeping Commitments

Joyce: It used to be that he would say good-bye to me and then be gone on some adventure for any length of time...sometimes many hours. By the time he would return I would be in a state of near panic.

I don't want to stop Barry from having his adventures because that is his nature, but having a time commitment helps me a lot. Even the two times that he climbed Mt. Shasta, once with our son, John-Nuri, for his thirteenth birthday, and the second time with John-Nuri and our daughter, Mira, he still gave me an approximate time line. He left in the afternoon and told me he would be back sometime in the evening of the following day.

At least once a year, he goes on some kind of solo wilderness adventure for a week or more. He needs this time as much as I need his promise to keep himself safe, and some kind of time line for his return.

There have been times when he has not been able to keep these commitments to me. Once, he was canoeing by himself and was not back at the agreed-upon time, which was three days after he left our home. He had no cell reception, his final day on the river had no current, and he couldn't make it to his take-out before dark. He was forced to find a campsite and spend an extra night on the river. He spent a troubled night knowing that I would be worried about him.

I remember lying in bed that night trying hard to trust that he would be okay. He told me before he left that the river was not dangerous. However, I decided that if one more day went by, I would initiate search and rescue.

Early the next morning, I received a phone call from Barry. He had hiked from his river campsite to an isolated farmhouse. The man actually came out with a shotgun pointing at him. Barry explained the situation, and the man pointed his gun away and invited Barry into his house where he could call me from a landline. He apologized for any worry the extra night had caused me. Keeping his body safe and keeping me informed are ways he loves me.

Taking Care of Your Body Too

Each morning we make green smoothies. I make mine first in a matter of minutes by basically just throwing in a big bunch of spinach, half an avocado, water and some fruit. Then Barry starts in on his "production." As I take my supplements, I watch with interest as he makes his smoothie. He puts in different kinds of fresh greens (sometimes picked from our garden minutes before), Swiss Chard, beet greens, kale, carrot tops, spinach, or anything else he can find. He wants to get the variety of nutrition from the different greens. Then he adds the other half of my avocado, dates, fresh ginger, almond milk and then some frozen fruit. He takes a long time to make his smoothie, blending thoroughly with each addition. I'm content with my spinach, and Barry never criticizes me for my simple smoothies, but I do enjoy watching him take good care of his body, partly as an expression of love for me.

I appreciate everything Barry does to take good care of his body. He exercises, gets enough sleep, drinks a lot of water and gets his blood tested each year. I want to be with him for as many years as possible. I feel loved every time he takes good care of his body.

Barry also maintains a good weight for him. Yes, he weighs a bit more than when he was a young man, but not by much. He asks me not to buy the vegan ice creams, cookies and other desserts that we both love. He knows he has trouble resisting them and they are gone almost as soon as they enter the house. By not eating desserts, we both are helped to keep our weight relatively down. Barry tries hard to keep his body as a "lover's body" for me and I appreciate that so much.

Barry loves me by encouraging me to also take good care of my body. He will suggest a longer walk than usual, getting to bed earlier and, my least favorite, fasting. I don't usually take him up on the fasting, but sometimes we go a whole day just drinking the green smoothies. By doing all that we can for our health, we are each showing the other that we care about our own bodies and want them to stay strong and healthy. That is a beautiful expression of love for ourself and each other.

To Really Appreciate a Woman

WOMEN AND MEN BOTH NEED APPRECIATION. By this we do not mean only compliments. Real appreciation is a gift of love straight from the heart, an acknowledgement of another's greatness and beauty, and a way of showing your partner that you really care.

What kind of appreciation does your woman need?

Many women need specific kinds of appreciation. And many men don't understand this. Here's an example:

Nick wanted Emma to know how physically beautiful she was. He appreciated her face, her hair, her breasts, her legs, and many other anatomical features. After each attempt at appreciation, Emma would slightly smile but say nothing. Nick shared his frustration about this, one day, in a couple's therapy session. I asked Emma the question Nick should have asked, "What kind of appreciation would feel the best to you?"

Emma hesitated at first to answer. She worried that telling Nick what she needed would be adding another chore to his "to-do" list. She may get the specific kind of appreciation she desired, but would it be real or forced? I encouraged her to take the risk anyway. Emma finally admitted that Nick's appreciation of her body did little for her. Because she had begun to develop early, her body had been the source of too much attention. She did not feel seen for who she was inside, her inner qualities and uniqueness. She started crying.

I noticed Nick's eyes were moist from hearing her emotional vulnerability, so I asked him to try a different way of appreciating Emma. He looked deeply into her eyes and began to speak, "Emma darling, you light up the room every time you enter... I love how you get enthusiastic like a little child about the simplest things in life. You bring magic and sparkle to my life..." Although he wasn't finished, Emma was now sobbing, so Nick reached out to hold her. He had just appreciated Emma in exactly the way she needed and wanted.

Some of this particular example can be gender-specific. Many women can relate to Emma's feelings about her body. Perhaps the deeper lesson here is about communication, taking the risk to find out from your partner what he or she really needs, rather than only trying to guess.

In most cases, it's fine to appreciate a woman's body *if* you also appreciate *who she is inside her body*. Too much focus on her body can give her the message that you want something (i.e. sex) from her, or that you don't care about her inner beauty.

> *I feel most loved by Jim when he so lovingly ad-*
> *mires those qualities in me that others have seen*
> *only in a negative light. For example, my devo-*
> *tion to being a good mother was seen by my*
> *daughter's dad as "over mothering," my*
> *strength has been perceived as nothing but*
> *stubbornness, my strong feelings as "too emo-*
> *tional," my shyness as arrogance.*
> *Because Jim sees the beauty in all of the quali-*
> *ties I have been led to believe were weaknesses, I*
> *feel that he is truly seeing and understanding*
> *me, allowing me to feel so deeply loved and ac-*
> *cepted.*
> —Rebecca Lipson, Tucson, AZ

Sean often said the words "I love you" to Erin. He felt this adequately expressed his love for her. Erin, however, needed more. She needed to hear what it was that Sean loved about her. The words "I love you" were nice but too vague. They lacked specifics. They could be said without real conviction or feeling. They could be said automatically.

It turns out that Sean, like many men, was uncomfortable expressing genuine appreciation. This truth came out during a workshop. "I love you" was really a token gesture, a cop-out from vulnerably letting Erin know what he loved about her.

With a little guidance, Sean was able to tell Erin, "I love how you feel everything so deeply. Sometimes I can't believe how lucky I am to be married to you."

Erin looked like a child on Christmas morning.

So if you find yourself only saying "I love you" to your partner, think details – what do you really love and appreciate about her. Remember, love is often in the details.

Josh often appreciated all the things Madison did for him, for the children, for the house, etc. He didn't understand how Madison felt trapped in the role of taking care of everyone and everything. For Madison, Josh's appreciation felt to her like an enabling of her dysfunction. It was a turn-off for her. What did she need instead? In her own words, "If only Josh could appreciate who I am rather than what I do. All my life, I was only praised for doing, or accomplishing, or achieving. If I'm not taking care of everyone, I feel worthless. But taking care of everyone, I still feel worthless. I feel trapped."

Madison was on the verge of crying, and her vulnerability opened Josh's heart. He held Madison and lovingly spoke, "Right now, right here, you don't have to *do* anything for me or anyone else. You deserve to be taken care of. Your beauty and goodness have nothing to do with what you do. I'm in love with who you are, not what you do." Those words triggered a flood of tears, because they came straight from Josh's heart, and were exactly what Madison needed to hear.

Your lesson as a man: many women can get trapped in the role of caregivers. Many women feel like a mother and often view their partner as another one of their children. If your partner is in this category, appreciate her childlike qualities like her innocence, her joy, her creativity, and especially her deserving love even when she does nothing. The highest appreciation in a case like this, more than the words, is to create the feeling in your partner that you are taking care of her, and doing it because it is your joy – rather than your duty.

> *I feel really loved by Jay when he says "I love you" or "I'm sorry" in the words that I understand and I use rather than the words he understands and uses.*
> – Cathleen Sullivan, Tinton Falls, NJ

Once again, find out what she needs rather than appreciating her in the way you need to be appreciated. For Nick, Emma's beauty was much more important to him than to her. But more to the point, his focus on her body reflected his own need to be validated as good-looking. In a previous book, *Light in the Mirror*, we demonstrated how our intimate partner is a mirror for us. The things we love about our partner are a reflection of our own goodness. The things we don't like about our partner are a reflection of the things we don't like about ourself. Projection is the psychological term for seeing parts of ourself in our partner, parts that may be invisible to us. In Nick's case, he was projecting his own need to be seen as handsome onto Emma. It was his need, not Emma's.

Sean's hollow "I love you" reflected his own lack of vulnerability, his discomfort with seeing what was loveable about himself, even his own discomfort with being seen, really seen.

Similarly, it was Josh's, and not Madison's, need to be appreciated for the things he did. Josh was the one who felt insecure about doing enough for Madison. Madison's insecurity was feeling trapped into doing too much for Josh and everyone else.

> *I may be having a difficult day where Prem and I may not see each other until late in the evening. He tenderly cups my face, looks deeply into my eyes, and says, "I love you." Then, after a pause, he says, "I REALLY love you!" It's something about the way he says it. At that moment, all of my doubt and insecurity is completely washed away.*
> –Liz Ellison, Felton, CA.

When you as a man can truly look at your loved one and see *her* rather than your own wishes, desires or fantasies, only then can you appreciate her for who she is, and only then will she feel appreciated. Every man can do this if he *wants* to. It doesn't require some magical quality or gift. You don't need to be a public speaker or a poet. You only need the courage to look at your beloved just a little closer, discover what is there in front of you, and then speak the words to describe what you see and feel. Most importantly, you need to desire to give her a gift, more than a physical one. Sure, giving her flowers, making her dinner, or arranging childcare is nice. But really seeing her, and appreciating her in the way she needs, will transform you from a regular husband into a real lover.

The Little Brown Book

Joyce: I love birthdays. I love to give cards and simple thoughtful presents and call people on their birthday. I also love it when people remember me on my birthday. When people send me cards or emails, I save them for a long time, reading them over and over again. When people call and wish me a happy birthday, I am apt to save the messages for many months. As nice as it is to receive love on my birthday, it gives me greater joy to give my love to people on their birthdays.

In 1976, I was a new mother with a seven-week-old baby girl, totally unprepared for how busy I would be. Sleepless nights had left me dragging around our little home yearning for even a little bit of relaxation. It was the day before Barry's birthday. Typically I would be able to shop for his present, make a special dinner or have exciting plans in order. I had nothing! What could I give him? I didn't have the strength to take our baby out shopping or make a nice dinner for him. We had been living on a simple diet of salads, brown rice and vegetables.

While I nursed Rami, I contemplated my dilemma. I loved doing arts and crafts and had plenty of supplies, but I knew Rami would not enjoy being put down long enough for me to even start something. What was I to do to honor the man I loved so much? After Rami finished nursing, I walked her around the house just looking around hoping to get ideas. My eyes happened to fall upon an old brown journal book my dad had given me, something that had been given to him long ago which he realized he would never use. The pages were blank and he thought I might like to write in it. I had stuck it in the bookshelf and forgotten about it. I took it out. It was a little musty, but ideas began to form in my mind.

On Barry's birthday, there was no special dinner and no exciting plans, but I did have a present all wrapped up. As Barry unwrapped it, he looked at me quizzically and said, "When did you have time to buy me a present?" He looked even more confused when he saw the old brown book. He opened it to the first page which read, "To my beloved Barry on your birthday. Your gift today is the gift of my words of love for you. Each and every year that I am able, I shall write in this book on your birthday to tell you how much I love you. I feel so deeply honored to be your wife and closest friend. I am so grateful to be sharing this life with you and now sharing the gift of parenting together..." I then went on to tell him all the things I appreciated about him. Barry loved this present so much that he asked if he could also write in it on my birthdays.

And that's how an unusual tradition has started. Each year on our birthdays we receive the gift of the old brown book. It now has many years of birthday entries and many years of appreciations and adoring messages. Barry is more of a poet than I am. He writes, "To see the petals of a rose unfold is to hint at the glory of your opening heart. Yet unlike the fully blossomed rose whose petals then begin to fall away, the petals of your heart keep opening wider and wider." My birthday messages are simpler, listing all the ways I appreciate him. The style really doesn't matter. What matters is that the book has become a treasured item. It truly gets richer and more meaningful year by year.

A few years ago, in June, our family was ordered by the county sheriff to evacuate our home due to an approaching wildfire. We had just a half hour to sort through all of our belongings and decide what we wanted to bring with us. Surprisingly our pile of stuff was very little: photos and art work by and of our children, a few clothes, a laptop computer and, of course, one important item – a shabby old brown book.

When my mother passed from this world to join my father, it was then up to me to sort through all of their stuff. My mother loved books and, as I was going through them all, I came across a little book with a smiley face on it. As I opened it I was drawn to the first page and a note from my mother, "Dear Joyce, I am starting to write in this little book shortly after you were born. I am going to write all the things I love about being your mother. Each page will be filled with my gratitude. I will try to always express this gratitude to you in words. However, someday you will not be able to hear my voice and I want you to know how much I love you and love being your mother." The book was filled with writings from my mother about her journey of parenting me. There were many physical things I inherited from my mother, but this little book with the smiley face upon it is by far the greatest.

Someday, after Barry and I have left this world, our three children will be sorting through our possessions. They will come to a little brown book that is not very attractive. Hopefully they will open it up and be able to read about two parents who deeply loved each other. I hope this book will be as much of a treasure to them as it has been to the two of us.

May 18, 1998

Thank you God, Great Spirit,
for the birth of my beloved,
for guiding us together eighteen years later,
and for bringing out the gifts
that we have to share with each other and the
world.
Joyce, you are a magnificent woman!
Remember in our early years
when I was embarrassed by how you walked?
Your walk really hasn't changed at all.
It is still just as childlike,
bouncy and exuberant.
But now it has other qualities added:
the grace of a queen,
the rhythm of a dancer,
the majestic power of a goddess,
and the compassion of a divine mother.

Your voice,
which I have always loved,
now is so much richer in tone.
Whether you choose to sing or not,
it doesn't matter,
your voice will always sing in my heart,
where it echoes endlessly like a great gong

waking up every cell in my body,
and a gentle tinkling bell reminding me of how
loved I am.

I especially want to honor you
for your unceasing desire for oneness with
spirit.
Even the pain it causes you
when you don't feel connected with God.
When you feel that pain,
you feel all the potential for true oneness,
you are in that moment joined with your high-
est self,
and you glow with a heavenly light.

In your deep desire for spiritual connection,
you are blessed among women.
I have been watching you for a while now this
morning,
sitting next to the Big Sur River,
reading some phrase or story in a book,
then closing your eyes to reflect,
to absorb the words God has to speak in your
heart.
You are the picture of serenity.
The sunlight dancing on the river,
the swift motion of the current,
are in contrast to the deep well of stillness in
your soul.

I can't imagine loving you any more than I do
in this moment,
but I know I will.

Happy birthday beloved.
Barry

To Really Choose a Woman

TO REALLY LOVE A WOMAN IS TO CHOOSE HER EVERY DAY. It's different from saying, "I love you." It's possible to love her and still not choose her. A woman needs to know that she is the one and only woman for you. It takes words and actions to show her that she is more special and important to you than other women.

Can One Person Choose the Relationship?

It was a difficult and painful counseling session. Ten days ago, Arnold had announced to Virginia that he was leaving their twenty-year marriage to be with another woman. Since that announcement, they had spent a number of sleepless nights painfully baring their souls. There was no question about their love for one another. Rather, Arnold revealed that he was not "in love" with Virginia. This was obviously painful to Virginia, who spent much of the session in tears.

Arnold revealed something significant to Joyce and me during the session. "I never really chose Virginia. She was always the one pursuing me. She asked me out on dates. She asked me to move in together. She asked me to marry her. True, I went along because I loved her, but she was the one who chose me all along. I know it hurts her deeply, but I'm finally choosing for myself, even though it's someone else."

I admit, it's not uncommon for one person to choose the relationship more than the other. But does it work? Not very well. In some ways, the person making the choice has more power. The person not making the choice has forfeited some of his or her power. The "chooser" is somewhat like a parent, while the chosen one becomes more of a child.

Especially when it comes to living together or marrying, both partners must equally choose, or the relationship is being built on a faulty and lop-sided foundation. Arnold admitted, "Virginia was the kindest, most loving woman I had ever met. It was the highest compliment that she wanted to be with me. I just couldn't say no to her choosing me. But now I know it was because I didn't think I would ever find as good a woman as her. That's not a good enough reason for a relationship. I feel like I've given her all my power by letting her choose me without my choosing her in return."

How I Chose Joyce

Now I need to be more personal. After three and a half years with Joyce, in the spring of 1968, she started bringing up marriage. Even though she never proposed to me, she made it clear that, for her, marriage was the next step. I, on the other hand, was content with having Joyce as my girlfriend. But underneath, I was really afraid to choose Joyce for the rest of my life. Marriage seemed too permanent ... too big a risk for me.

To her credit, rather than asking me to marry her, she made plans to move on with her life. She was soon graduating from Columbia Nursing School in New York City. She applied and was accepted as a nurse to work with Native Americans on a reservation in the southwest, thousands of miles from New York. I remember feeling that she would never leave me. How could she? She loved me too much. So I maintained my stance of inactivity, in a way calling her bluff.

The next day she announced she had just bought a one-way plane ticket. In those days, tickets were fully refundable, but I started to get nervous anyway. Joyce really was moving on with her life without me. If I wasn't going to choose her, she was choosing a career away from me. My indecision was too painful to her.

I spent a few days examining my deepest feelings. I certainly didn't want to choose to marry Joyce just because she was leaving, yet I did feel sorrow at the thought of losing her. I allowed my mind to play out my life without

Joyce. It became unbearable. I felt that losing Joyce would be the greatest mistake of my life. In that moment, in my mind and heart, I chose to spend the rest of my life with Joyce.

The next day, I went out and ordered a diamond engagement ring. It would cost me every penny I had, but I would be choosing Joyce, and that was worth everything. I wanted it to be a surprise, but made the mistake of telling my mother, who was never good with secrets.

A week later, Joyce and I stopped by my family home. As we opened the door and went inside, my mother blurted out, "Barry, the jeweler called to say the ring is ready."

Her hand then went quickly to her mouth.

"Oops, I shouldn't have said that..."

I saw the beginnings of a smile form on Joyce's lips, but nobody said anything more. I did, however, notice my older sister, Donna, shoot an exasperated glance at my mother.

The next day, I picked up the ring, stowed it safely in my pocket, then drove down into New York City to be with Joyce. From her dormitory at the Columbia Presbyterian Medical Center, we walked to our favorite place, the George Washington Bridge. We ventured out to the first tower and there, hundreds of feet above the Hudson River, I took the ring from my pocket and asked Joyce to marry me. She looked down at the ring in my hand and felt two things: first, a resounding YES, and second, fear that I might drop the ring. We were standing on a walkway grate with holes easily big enough for a ring to fall through and be lost forever. No matter, the important thing was that I chose Joyce to be my wife.

Choosing a Woman Over Your Mother

There are several things that can get in the way of a man's conscious choosing of a woman. Too many men hold onto an unhealthy choosing of their mothers. It is often unconscious, and can even be present when he dislikes his mother, and feels guilty about it. Most women are ultrasensitive to this ambivalence. When she feels you putting your mother first, it is painful to her.

The mother-son bond is powerful. Joyce and I understand the strong love of a mother with her son. The problem is the often-unconscious codependence that goes along with this unique bond of love. If a mother does not have a deep love and connection with a man, it can be too easy to transfer some elements of an unfulfilled adult relationship onto her son. In a way then, her son becomes a little like a lover, filling a void in her life. Most mothers would never consciously do this. They would recognize that this is hurtful to their sons. But, alas, we are not conscious all the time.

You, as men, may need your woman's help to break away from an unhealthy mother bond. You may not know when you are putting your mother's needs above your partner's needs. If she tells you she feels uncomfortable with something concerning your mother, don't ignore it.

Don't ever assume she is being too jealous, insecure, or making too much out of something trivial. Better still, ask her first if something you are planning with your mother feels OK with her. And always, ask yourself in any situation with your mother if you are choosing your partner first. If you're not sure you are choosing your partner first, you probably aren't.

I had this problem with Joyce early in our relationship. And I sometimes didn't know when I was choosing my mother over Joyce. In fact, we had problems just about every time we visited my childhood home. Joyce has told me that she could actually feel me change into a different person (and not someone she particularly liked) even when we turned onto the street leading to our house. And it got worse when we actually entered the house! I often ignored her when I was with my mom. It would be so painful to Joyce that she sometimes had to leave the house. When I went out to find her, she would be angry and I would be in denial that I did anything wrong. Not a pretty scene!

As the years passed, I learned that I had some responsibility in what happened, especially in how I acted when around Joyce and my mom. Before visiting my family home, Joyce and I would have a pep talk, and I would walk into the house more prepared. This preparation helped me keep from changing into another person for longer and longer with each visit. But inevitably, I would revert back into my mother's little boy, and gone was the man that Joyce loved.

I learned two important things that really helped me. One was that I still had unconscious dependence upon my mother. A very young part of me would actually walk into the house wanting my mommy. The whole environment, the smells of her cooking, the sound of her voice, the familiar surroundings, the furniture, all of it conspired in my regression to a small child.

My second revelation was even harder to process. I was afraid of hurting my mother. I was afraid of the pain I would cause her by choosing Joyce over her. But I knew I had to do just that, and if it hurt my mom, then it was a necessary pain.

The final victory, however, was my conscious choosing of Joyce over my mother. Joyce never wanted me to stop loving my mother. That was not the point. She just wanted me to stop making my mother's needs more important than hers. I had to learn, especially in my early individuation phase, to check in with Joyce often when I was in the presence of my mom. This was my way of letting Joyce know I was choosing her.

I remember an important moment during our first pregnancy. My parents were visiting our home. Joyce and I were in the living room when my mom entered the room. She began, "I want to tell you both how to give a proper Jewish name to a child…"

In my peripheral vision, I caught the painful look on Joyce's face. I knew I had to act quickly.

"Mom," I interrupted, "first of all, Joyce is not Jewish. And second, the two of us will be coming up with our own name for our child, a name that feels good to both of us."

I could see the painful look on my mother's face as she realized I was choosing my wife first and foremost. If there can ever be healthy pain, this was it. I could see her letting go of me, her son, ever so slightly. I could also see her opening up in that moment to Joyce as the most important person in my life. If I were choosing Joyce, then she would have to as well.

Most importantly, however, whenever we got together with my parents, I made it a point to tell my mother how much I loved Joyce and how important she was to me. This was often not easy for my mother to hear, but it truly gave her the message that Joyce was now my priority. And, because she saw how important Joyce was to me, she and Joyce were able to establish a new and loving relationship of their own. The visits lost the tension that had been there, and actually became fun.

Currently, my mom is ninety-five. And to show you how different things have become, my mom has pronounced more than once, "Barry, you know that Joyce is the best thing that has ever happened to you!" And I smile in agreement.

Choosing a Woman Over All Other Women

It's also vitally important to choose your woman over all other women. For some men, this is not as easy as it sounds. Take Jack for example. He met and began a relationship with Audrey while visiting a friend in Philadelphia. After several more visits to be with her, and one month where she lived with him in his home-town of Boston, she decided to move in with him. Red flag number one: she chose him, and sacrificed for him.

Now it was time for Audrey to officially meet Jack's friends, most of whom were women, and some from childhood. He had a party and invited all his friends to welcome Audrey to Boston, and into his life. Red flag number two: at the party, Jack spent most of his time with his friends, leaving Audrey to fend for herself. He figured she would have the chance to introduce herself around. He didn't really understand that Audrey, being an introvert, instead sat by herself on a couch in the corner of the room, feeling abandoned. Jack also didn't understand the message he broadcast to all of his friends that evening: that Audrey was less important to him than they were.

From that evening on, Jack's friends made no real effort to welcome Audrey into their circle. Why should they. If she wasn't that important to him, then she wasn't worthy of their effort either. Some of his friends openly showed their dislike of Audrey by ignoring or being rude to her. Audrey, meanwhile, was ready to pack it up and move back to Philadelphia.

Joyce and I encouraged Jack to make a strong stand for Audrey. His first attempt fell short. "Audrey," he began, "you know how much I love you. My friends are also important, and I don't want to lose them."

Audrey, to her credit, stood up for herself, and said, "When you say that, it sounds like your friends are more important than I am, that you're more afraid of losing them than me."

Jack looked sad and I intervened. "Listen, Jack. If you continue to choose your friends, even just as much as you choose Audrey, you will definitely lose Audrey. If you choose Audrey as the most important person in your life, you may lose some of your friends. They may feel replaced and hurt. But there's a chance that some of your friends will grow into even better friends by understanding the healthy choice you have made."

In the Disney movie, *The Lion King*, Simba, the young lion, had a comfortable life with his two friends, Timon, the meerkat, and Pumbaa, the warthog. Their theme song, "Hakuna Matata," meant "no worries." Enter Nala, the young lioness love interest. Timon and Pumbaa at first lament the loss of their friend. It's clear that Simba is choosing Nala over them. Okay, it's just one song, "Can You Feel the Love Tonight," but in a musical, a lot can happen in one song. Timon and Pumbaa rally, however, because they know Simba needs their friendship, and help to reclaim the pride lands from Simba's evil uncle, Scar. They learn to accept that Simba's and Nala's primary relationship is more important than the original three friends.

No, I didn't tell Jack the story of the Lion King, but I didn't need to. He got it on his own. He made the right choice. And yes, he did lose some of his friends, the ones who were unwilling to grow into a new relationship with Jack. But other friends are even better friends today. They were able to sacrifice the original friendship to have an even deeper friendship now. And Jack and Audrey have new friends, including couple friends, who are happy to get to know them as a couple.

> *I've always longed for someone to make room in their lives for me. When I made the decision to leave Alaska and to move in with my new husband, it was truly scary for me. When I arrived at his house, I found he had cleaned half of the closet for me, and half of the dresser. He was making room in his life for me.*
> –Joy Davis, Centralia, WA.

I remember a time, in 1975, at a Sufi camp with Pir Vilayat Khan in the French Alps, where I fell into the role of camp doctor. During a meal in the beginning of the camp, a woman approached me in a moment when I was not near Joyce. Someone had pointed me out as the doctor, and she had a medical question. But it wasn't that simple. I remember she was standing a little too close to me, yet I didn't back up to adjust the distance. And there was more than a hint of flirtatiousness, which I likewise did nothing about.

At that moment, Joyce came up beside me, more than likely guided by her intuition. I missed it, but Joyce later said the woman had a look of irritation when she saw Joyce at my side. After several minutes, the woman looked at Joyce and impatiently asked, "Do you want something?"

Joyce answered, "I'm Barry's wife!"

The woman was clearly embarrassed and said, "I didn't know Barry was married." She quickly left.

What did I do wrong? One, I ignored the woman's physical proximity and inappropriate energy. Two, I made matters worse by not putting my arm around Joyce as soon as she joined me and introducing her as my wife to this woman. I actually ignored my wife's presence. I didn't know it at the time, but there was a part of me that was enjoying the exclusive attention of this woman, not aware of how hurtful this was to Joyce. In that one interaction, I was unintentionally choosing the other woman over Joyce.

Now, I am so comfortable choosing Joyce that my arm is almost constantly around her when we are with other people. Nobody ever gets the message that they are more important than Joyce. And I believe it makes people feel more comfortable. They clearly know my choice and there-fore can relax. There's no question about my allegiance.

You also choose her by remaining free of addictions. It doesn't matter what kind of addiction you have. Any addiction, whether it be alcohol, pot, other drugs, food, sex, or work, is a way you do not choose her. Addiction is running away from your emotions, and running away from your emotions is running away from your relationship. Most men understand this running away in every case of addiction – except pot addiction. Because of this lack of understanding, pot addiction is often the most insidious destroyer of relationships.

We have counseled many couples where one partner (usually the man) was habitually using pot. In each case, there was much pain and disconnection. We have seen that even once a week use on a Saturday night can block intimacy during the rest of the week.

The nature of intimacy ("into me see") is being able to see into your partner and to allow your partner to see into you *clearly*. We have seen that marijuana blocks a clear perception of your deeper feelings and of your partner's needs in the relationship, while at the same time it gives a false sense of heightening these same qualities. This is why it is one of the most dangerous substances for relationship, as well as the most well-defended by its users. If you are using pot, you may feel that everything is fine in your relationship, or that the pot use is one of the things that is helping, rather than hindering, your connection with your partner. The "sacred herb," as it is sometimes erroneously called, is, on the contrary, preventing you from feeling your own as well as your partner's deeper feelings, especially sadness and pain. If you use pot, even occasionally, you are running away from "unpleasant" feelings. True growth can only occur when you are willing to feel all your feelings, to sit with them, to learn from them, to follow them through to real healing and resolution.

If you are the pot-free partner, you may find yourself feeling abandoned often without a clue, and often blaming yourself as the cause. Or pot becomes the "other" woman with whom your partner is having an affair ... even an occasional affair. You may feel intense feelings of jealousy or rage and, because your partner has not been with another person, you judge yourself more severely for having these feelings. Even when you ask your partner to choose between you and pot, they assure you they are choosing you because they really believe they are. Yet their continued use of pot is evidence to the contrary. Your work in this type of relationship is to look deeply inside to see how you are not honoring yourself. You may think you deserve better, but your feelings may tell you otherwise.

We have seen problems with pot addiction worked out in several ways. The best is when the couple realizes that pot is blocking their intimate connection. They can then seek help either through counseling, recovery programs or, ideally, both. The challenge can be handled by both partners within the context of the relationship, each looking deeply at their own contribution to the problem, rather than blaming the other partner.

If the marijuana user remains in denial, then the only alternative is for the pot-free partner to leave. This allows the user to more clearly face their relationship with pot, to decide if this really has been their relationship of choice. Being left often shocks a user into reality. Is my pot habit worth losing my partner or family? We have seen individuals at this point eventually seek the help that they need. We have seen couples come back together and work together to heal the underlying dysfunction in their relationship.

The saddest situation is when the pot-free partner tries to patiently wait, sometimes year after year, for their partner to give up their habit. This person is settling for second best and trying to make the best out of it. They usually end up pouring their energy and attention into the children, their career, or their friends, while trying to keep a lid on their growing resentment. The intimacy of this couple is severely handicapped as they are both settling for less than real love. Their chances for survival as a couple are poor.

A deep, loving, passionate and fulfilling relationship is one of the great gifts of this life. It can bless you, your partner, your children, your work in the world, and your health. Why put anything into your body that would rob you of this great happiness? When you are addiction-free, you can finally really choose her.

Choosing a Woman Over Your Career

Are your work and career more important than your relationship? Your work is often strongly linked to your providing for your woman and family. But if your work becomes a stronger choice than your relationship, she will feel replaced, rejected and not as important. She may feel that your work is your primary relationship ... even your mistress.

During Barry's fourth year of medical school at USC in Los Angeles, I was able to land a dream job. I was the head nurse in charge of a new residential treatment program for boys. The facility was a beautiful three-thousand-acre ranch donated by Cecil B. DeMille, the famous movie-maker. Since part of my responsibility involved hiring the staff, I naturally hired many of my friends. The staff of thirty became like a warm and loving family not only to the boys, but to me as well. I had never before known such joy in a job, never realized it was possible to laugh and play at work. Since Barry was often busy working at the hospital, I stayed longer and longer hours at work. I found I was happier there than I was alone at home. Yet, however fulfilled I felt by this dream job, Barry always remained my first choice.

I'll never forget the evening I came home from a truly joyful day at work. Barry greeted me with a big smile and said, "I've been accepted for my residency in psychiatry at the University of Oregon Medical Center in Portland. We'll need to move in two months."

Of course, I was happy for Barry's acceptance, but there was something about the way he announced "our" move to Portland. There was no asking, or other consideration of my feelings. It felt in a way like he was choosing the next step in his career over me and our relationship.

My heart sank. I didn't want to leave. For the first time in my life I was truly happy in my work. I felt needed, important and loved. I couldn't bear to leave my job. I knew this residency offer was important to Barry, but I was tired of following him around the country, tired of making all the sacrifices for his education. I left my family and my first nursing job in Buffalo, New York, to move to Nashville, Tennessee, for Barry to start medical school. Then, two years later, I left my public health job in Nashville to move with him to Los Angeles to finish medical school. I had sacrificed enough for Barry!

I blurted out, "I'm not going with you!"

I was actually surprised at the bold stand I was taking.

After our initial shock, a respectful and loving silence surrounded us as we both pondered my decision. We talked of frequent visits back and forth, and of Barry returning to Los Angeles after the three-year residency.

Two weeks later, I returned home from work to find Barry waiting for me. He seemed peaceful and resolved when he spoke, "I decided to give up my residency program. It's more important for me to stay here with you. You're more important than my career. I'll find a job here in LA, then reapply next year for a local residency."

I was in awe at the choice Barry had just made for our relationship – for me! He and I both knew that without an internship his medical education was practically worthless. His choice of job might include working as a laboratory assistant. He was willing to give up at least a year of his life just to be with me! I could tell this choice had come from a place deep inside of him. He was at peace and I felt profound respect for him.

One week later, my own decision came from a similar inner place of peace. I gave notice at my job and prepared to move fifteen hundred miles away to Portland, Oregon.

Barry actually tried to stop me from doing this. "Joyce," he pleaded, "You've always chosen me first. Give me this chance to choose you, to show you that you're most important in my life."

I smiled, "Right now, I feel completely chosen by you. You made your decision to choose me. That's all I needed and wanted. Please let me now choose you over my own career."

I often reflect on that time in our marriage. Without a willingness on both of our parts to choose our relationship over our careers, our marriage might not have survived. Our careers were already trying to take priority over our marriage. Now a new precedent was set. Our marriage and family would remain our first choice for the rest of our lives.

I Choose You!

It was the morning of June 26, 2010. A sound system was being set up for our daughter's wedding outside our house, with speakers big enough to handle a rock concert. I was taking care of a last-minute request to clear poison oak on the lower part of our sixteen acres, where the reception would follow. I was hundreds of feet from our house and normally far from earshot.

Joyce was asked to say the most important thing from her heart into the microphone to test the sound system. Imagine my surprise when I hear her voice broadcast over, not only our property, but also the neighbor's in every direction, "BARRY, WHEREVER YOU ARE, I CHOOSE YOU ALL OVER AGAIN. I WOULD MARRY YOU AGAIN IN A SECOND!"

I cup my hands to my mouth and call out in the loudest voice I can muster, "JOYCE, I WILL ALWAYS CHOOSE YOU!"

And she heard me! So did a lot of other people, but that didn't matter. What mattered most is that we have been choosing each other almost daily. It's become one of our most endearing practices, and one that we highly recommend to other couples.

To Really Listen to a Woman

A BEAUTIFUL WAY THAT A MAN LOVES A WOMAN IS TO SIMPLY LISTEN TO HER. It sounds like such an easy thing to do, but in reality it can sometimes be the most difficult thing.

Barry and I have dear friends, Pat and Judy, whom we have known for many years. Before he died, Pat worked as a fireman for thirty years until he retired. He was an excellent fireman, always helpful, efficient in getting the job done, kind and compassionate to those he was there to serve. He was devoted to his wife.

Sometimes Judy would have a problem and she would want Pat to listen to her. Pat would hear the words "problem" or "challenge" and would immediately go into his fireman role. He would try to put out the fire. Judy, on the other hand, just wanted Pat to sit down and listen to her. By telling her beloved husband about her challenge, she felt she could gain insight just by the reflection of his listening. This had always been a problem for them. Judy wanted Pat to listen. Pat wanted to put out the "fire" for her as soon as possible. He offered suggestions, solutions, and advice.

I happened to be with them one time and, with my help, Pat had an epiphany. He understood what Judy needed. Astonished, he looked at me and remarked, "You mean all I have to do is sit there and listen to Judy! That's

134   VISSELL

all! I don't have to do anything to fix the situation? That's too easy!"

I suggested that he hold her hand, look into her eyes, and focus on what she was feeling rather than what he could do to fix her problem. Then perhaps the most important words he could speak would be, "I understand," or "Judy, you have a right to feel these feelings."

Pat smiled and said, "I was trying too hard, and in all the wrong ways. All I have to do is listen. I don't have to be a fireman."

One of the greatest gifts you can offer your woman is to just be there and listen. Along with listening, it's important to trust that she can handle the situation on her own. Simply listening gives a positive message that you support her by believing in her own ability.

A few years before his death, my beloved father was hospitalized with a pulmonary embolism. He came close to dying, and it was a scary time for our family. Since he was totally deaf, I felt that someone from the family should be with him at all times during the day. Doctors and nurses would come in and shout at him in loud voices, thinking they could get him to hear them. My father didn't know what was going on, so he would pretend to understand and agree to things he didn't want. I explained that he didn't hear anything, but they still insisted they could get through to him. My mother and brother went in together for half the time, and I covered the rest.

After four days of this, I felt so sad to see my father so sick and I felt discouraged at the insensitivity toward him in the hospital. Before I went to be with him that day, I started telling Barry how I felt. He immediately went into his medical doctor role and started suggesting better care for my father. This is not what I needed! There was a tense moment between us and I must have expressed my disappointment. Barry felt hurt because he felt he was trying to help. I left with tears in my eyes.

When I returned home that night, Barry held me and asked me to tell him what was going on. He simply sat, held me, and let me express my sadness over my dad's condition, and my anger over the way he was being treated by the hospital staff. Barry just listened to me for half an hour. I felt so close and grateful. That half hour helped me to get through several more difficult days until we could bring my dad home again. By Barry taking the time to just listen to me, I felt supported in my feelings. I was able to take in his love and caring and thus receive enormous strength.

Listening to the woman in your life is a precious gift. If she will let you hold her while she talks, that has the potential to make the time even more powerful. There is no need to give advice, unless she asks for that. Just sit and listen and let your love pour into her in a quiet way. She will be so grateful.

> *I feel really loved by Scott when he gently caresses me and says "Honey, how are you?" And when I look in his eyes I see that he **really** wants to know.*
> –Venus Elyse, Fairfax, CA

Listen to the Goddess

To really love a woman is to listen to her deeply. Of course, it's wonderful to understand her words and reflect back this understanding to her, but I'm speaking about a deeper listening. I love listening to the goddess expressing through Joyce. Sometimes it can be words that soothe and comfort the hurting little boy within me. Sometimes it can be words that penetrate my defenses when I've put up a wall between us during an argument. Other times it can be words that wake me up from an unconscious slumber, helping me to see the truth in a situation.

Often it's not words, but the sounds of the goddess, like the true joy of her laughter, the complete letting go with reckless abandon, not caring who hears or judges. In fact, it was this laughter that first attracted me to Joyce when we were but children of eighteen years. We were in our first year at Hartwick College in Oneonta, New York. It was a brisk autumn day at a soccer game. I was sitting in the stands with my friends, trying to act more grown up than I was. That meant controlled laughter ... not too loud ... and controlled body movements ... never anything that could be judged as childish. After all, I was eighteen years old going on thirty.

A couple of rows above and behind me, the loud noise of laughter kept me from concentrating on the game. Annoyed, but also curious, I turned around to see what was going on. I saw Joyce for the first time, sitting with her friends and laughing the "wrong" way ... way too loud, uncontrolled, obviously immature, and worst of all, not caring at all what people must be thinking of her. How dare she act so childish! But I couldn't stop looking at her. My mind was repelled by her, but my heart, which I scarcely understood at the time, was irresistibly attracted to her. I was having minimal fun. Joyce was having all the fun she wanted. I was dampening my joy. Joyce was freeing hers. I was hiding my childlikeness. Joyce was in no hurry to grow up, exuberant in her innocence.

Unbeknownst to me, that day at the soccer game, I had started to fall in love with Joyce. The goddess knows how to play. It has taken me years to learn from the goddess. She has taught me well. I learned to occasionally (okay, maybe more than occasionally) act completely silly and truly not care what people think, and I have been judged by some for this. Maybe I'm just making up for lost time.

And all this just because I first heard her laughing above me in the bleachers!

> *One time my mate asked me, "what would you like for gifts on your birthdays?" I gave him a list for the next ten years. On my next birthday he gave me everything on that list!!*
> –Laurie Moore, Santa Cruz, CA

But You Can't Always Listen to Her

What happens when Joyce needs me to listen to her, and I am not in the proper frame of mind? This has been a disaster in our earlier years. I have sometimes tried to listen to her when my attention simply wasn't with her. Rather than telling her that I couldn't listen at that particular moment, that I was focusing all my energy on something else, I instead tried to be present. Unconsciously, I feel that it is a sign of weakness to not be fully available to my beloved at all times. After all, Super Husband can be constantly emotionally present!

Here's how it looks:

I'm sitting in the office, deeply focused on some project. Joyce enters.

"Barry, can I talk with you about something?"

"Sure."

Joyce talks for about two minutes.

"Barry, are you sure you can give me your attention right now?"

"Sure."

Joyce talks for another two minutes.

"Barry, I don't feel you're with me. It's starting to hurt my feelings."

"But I'm trying, Joyce!"

And then it can quickly get ugly, with Joyce feeling more hurt, me feeling more defensive, and both of us getting angry.

Now here's how I love Joyce in the same situation:

Same scenario, I'm deeply focused in the office, and Joyce enters.

"Barry, can I talk with you about something?"

"Can it wait? I'm really focused on finishing a project. This is not a good time for me, but as soon as I'm done, I can give you my full attention."

If it's urgent, she will tell me and I will stop everything to be with her. But if it's not urgent, she would rather have me be fully present later, than partially present now. She feels loved by my honesty and healthy boundaries.

> *Charlie loves me by listening when I go on and on at length about something that is bothering me, and doesn't try to fix me or the situation. He listens respectfully, sometimes asking the best questions that help me clarify what is true for me, while I find my own way to a solution.*
> – Linda Bloom, Santa Cruz, CA

Honoring and Protecting a Woman's Sensitivity

BARRY REALLY LOVES ME BY HONORING AND PRO-
TECTING MY SENSITIVITY. I'm learning to protect and accept this quality myself, but it's also so special to have him
accept and guard my sensitivity.

I have all of the qualities of a highly sensitive person.
When I was young, I was ashamed of these qualities. Now
I'm learning that it's part of my beauty as a human being.
Barry has helped me so much by his acceptance.

I grew up with my mother, father, and a brother four
years older than me. My brother was tested as genius intelligence and, even as a child, was on his way to becoming a
world famous electrical engineer. My dad was also a brilliant engineer. Though I got excellent grades in school, my
greater strength was my emotional intelligence. This is a
quality that today is beginning to be recognized. Back in
the early fifties, it was not. My family did not know what
to do with a child that cried and showed emotion. I was
easily hurt by what my brother considered "harmless teasing." This teasing would usually happen during mealtime
when I was young. My brother would say something to me
that he thought was funny, but I would feel hurt. I would

start to cry and my dad would say, "Joyce, you're too sensitive. You've got to learn to take a joke."

Or a family member would be "silently" angry in the house and no one would feel it but me. I would say something, or even begin to cry, and again I was told by my father, "Joyce, you're too sensitive. You won't be able to make it when you grow up. You have to overcome this."

I loved my dad. And I knew his engineering mind was trying to fix me rather than understand my sensitive nature. He sincerely wanted the best life for me and was a good father in many ways. He simply didn't understand sensitivity and saw mine as a huge stumbling block to my happiness in the world.

By the time I met Barry while living in college away from my parents' home, I felt that my sensitivity was a huge handicap. Some people are blind. Some are deaf or paralyzed. I was *sensitive*! My sensitivity felt like a heavy burden. I felt ashamed to be so sensitive. Even as a young eighteen-year-old, Barry helped me realize that I could not get rid of this inner quality, that I needed to accept myself just as I am. For the first time in my life, I heard words from him that I had been longing for my whole life, "Joyce, I feel your sensitivity is beautiful." Simple words and yet they meant so much. Could it possibly be true that my sensitivity is actually beautiful? Those first spoken words of acceptance forty-nine years ago started me on my path of accepting my sensitivity and realizing that it is one of the most beautiful parts of who I am. Those seven words had a profound effect on me, but just as a thirsty person is not satisfied with only one drink of water, I needed to hear those words over and over again.

There are times when accepting my sensitivity is relatively easy. When we are leading workshops, I can sense participants' needs and understand their feelings. When our three children were living at home, I could feel what was troubling them sometimes even before they realized it. When I am out in my garden, I can sense what each plant needs. I am also sensitive to Barry's thoughts and feelings. I can hear the spiritual voice of my heart, my intuition, speaking silently to me. These parts of my sensitivity are beautiful for me.

But Barry helps me with harder parts of being sensitive. I can feel the energy of the person who has written me a letter or email. This is most often a lovely feeling. However, when someone is writing because they are angry, even if they don't express it in words, these angry feelings go right into my body like a poison. Close friends know that emailing or writing to me about negative feelings is not a good way to communicate with me. The biggest problems are writings from someone who is blaming one of us for something that has come up for them in a workshop or counseling experience.

For example, a woman felt safe enough during a workshop to tell her husband that she had been having an affair with another man. Her husband was naturally shocked but, after the workshop, he wrote an angry letter blaming us for ruining his marriage. The anger was obviously at his wife but, because he was addressing all of this anger toward me, it went through my body like a poison. I actually felt sick for hours. Because Barry is not as affected by other people's anger, I have learned now to have him screen all such potential writings by reading them first. He will then describe the content to me in his own words, acting like a filter for me.

I even feel energies in a room from former occupants. It's difficult for me to stay in hotels because of the large number of recent occupants, so Barry has accepted that we try to find other alternatives for sleeping arrangements when traveling, usually someone's home. If we have to stay in a hotel, Barry will help me by calling to the angels to clear any negative emotions from the room. This really helps me to more easily sleep.

If we are in a social situation with a lot of people and someone becomes angry, I will feel it. Sometimes we are able to help shift the energy back to positive. If not, and there is still negativity in the area, it is painful to stay in such a situation. Barry will leave with me, even if he doesn't necessarily want to.

Barry helps me with my sensitivity by sitting in the middle seat on airplanes, creating a buffer between me and another passenger. Let's face it, the middle seat of a three-seat row in economy is not most people's idea of a good time, but Barry does this willingly. I have also flown countless times by myself, even to Europe three times alone, but this small act of courtesy to protect my sensitivity when we are flying together means so much to me.

Because Barry cannot always be there to help me when my sensitivity seems overwhelming to me, I have also learned to comfort myself. When I start to feel ashamed of my sensitivity and hear my father's voice saying, "Joyce, you are too sensitive," I put my arms around myself and start to talk to myself. "Joyce, I love that you are so sensitive. This is your greatest strength. Yes, it hurts sometimes, but it's part of your beauty. There's nothing wrong with you. Your sensitivity is beautiful." I keep up these inner messages until I no longer feel ashamed of my feelings.

But the most beautiful thing that Barry does for me is to hold me and let me know that my sensitivity is beautiful. Just recently, I listened to our office answering machine and was surprised to hear an angry message from a person I knew well. This took me by total surprise. I tried calling this person back but he had left for the day. I was left with the poison of the angry words and I started to cry.

Barry was in New York City visiting with his mother and answered when I called him. I was crying. Right away he said, "Remember, Joyce, your sensitivity is so beautiful. I really love that about you so much."

After we talked for a few more minutes, I felt better. His voice of love and assurance is always so comforting and healing for me. He has also shared with me that my sensitivity has blessed his life as well. It has given him permission to open more to his own deeper sensitivity.

Through Barry's help I now know that I am not too sensitive. No one is. I am *beautifully sensitive*. My feelings have been given to me as a gift. Yes, there are challenges in this world for the sensitive person, but the positive aspects of being sensitive far surpass the negative. I am so grateful for my husband's love, acceptance and understanding in this process of healing my shame of being too sensitive.

If you are with a woman who is highly sensitive and deeply feels her feelings, you are blessed indeed. This woman can help to change your life in such a positive way. The more you can acknowledge the beauty of her sensitivity, the more she will be able to use her sensitivity to love you.

July 3, 2005

To my beloved Joyce,
I feel so privileged just to be in your presence.
I am a deeply blessed man to have found and
recognized you.
I honor your deep sensitivity.
You have always been my teacher in this area.
You sometimes joke or wish you could be more
like me
and not feel everything so deeply.
But I want to be more like you
and feel the depth and richness of all my feel-
ings.
This earth and all its people need most what
you have.
Your sensitivity is the heart of compassion,

its deepest essence.
Your sensitivity is the cornerstone of your intu-
ition,
the divine guidance for your life
as well as the healing of so many others.
Your sensitivity is a rare, fragrant and beauti-
ful rose
which those, blinded by their pain,
try to trample but never succeed
because your sensitivity is your soul,
and it cannot be touched,
except by gentleness and love.
Your sensitivity is childhood's innocence,
motherhood's nurturing blessing,
a woman's finest gift to a man,
and the heart of the goddess.
Thank you, my beloved Joyce,
for teaching me all these things about sensitiv-
ity,
and allowing me to honor this in you.
Barry

Honoring Her Need To Be Alone

SOME PEOPLE HAVE A GREAT NEED TO BE ALONE TO REPLENISH THEMSELVES. In order to be peaceful and happy with others, they must first be alone. Once this need is met, they can then be with other people.

Others receive energy from being around people. When they are not physically with people, they will make phone calls so they can feel the connection over the phone. In order to feel peaceful and happy in their lives, this need for contact with others must be met.

People fall into one of these two categories to a lesser or greater extent. Some people love to be around others for weeks on end, but then will have a need to be totally alone. Some people can be totally alone for weeks and then have an overwhelming urge to be around people as much as they can.

I fall into the first category. I have a great need to be alone, at least part of every day. Early in the morning, I have a spiritual time in silence during which I read something inspiring, pray and do my Tai Chi. Typically I receive a beautiful peace from this time alone which stays with me for quite a while during the day. Without this time to myself, I cannot function very well.

Barry understands this need, so it's rarely an issue in our relationship. I go to great lengths to be able to have my alone time, especially when we are traveling and it can be a challenge for me to have an extra half hour by myself.

Once we were teaching at a conference center in Germany and were given a tiny bedroom in which there was barely enough room for the two of us to walk past each other. I did my Tai Chi moves over the bed. Knowing how important this quiet spiritual time is for me, Barry looked out the window and considered walking in the icy rain. Instead, he opted for a little corner of the room, put on his earphones, turned on a Hawaiian song on his iPod, and practiced hula dancing which he loves so much. As I write this, I'm smiling as I picture him facing the corner, silently practicing a hula move while waiting for me to finish my Tai Chi.

As part of loving me, Barry has had to understand my deep need to be alone. Except when we are traveling, the morning time flows very well, but sometimes I also have a need to be alone for our morning walk with our dogs. I know Barry would usually prefer to walk with me and, when we do, it's a lot of fun. But there are some days when my need for solitude is so great that I have to tell him I will be walking alone.

It was not always easy for me to make this request of him. Years ago, when I first felt this need for solitude, I felt awkward asking Barry to walk alone, and I would take a different trail. My awkwardness and fear of hurting Barry's feelings would sometimes come across badly, and his feelings would often be hurt. Sometimes, I hate to admit, I would pick a fight with him so that I could be alone. Of course, this was unhealthy and made us both feel bad.

So, as I've accepted my need, I've learned to lovingly ask for more time to be alone. And Barry never knows when I'll ask for this. He's learned to accept this part of me, that my need to be alone has nothing to do with him. My need to be alone is just my need to be alone. It's not my need to be away from him. Sometimes my need for aloneness can be satisfied by walking together in silence. This is something we both like very much.

Seven times a year we have groups come to our home for workshops. Some of the groups last four days, and people are everywhere in our home, including sleeping in our living room. Besides the workshop in the living room, we also prepare meals with everyone and eat together. Before the people come, I make sure to have plenty of time alone to fill up my "alone savings account." But sometimes it gets too much for me and I will skip lunch to go swimming at the local fitness club. This place is not fancy, but it does have a nice outdoor pool. Once I get into the pool and begin my hour-long swim, no one can talk to me and my need to be alone is fulfilled. Barry stays back home and gets the lunch on the table and eats with the rest of the group. He knows I will come back a much happier person.

In one of our couple's workshops, we met a woman who felt ashamed of her need to be alone. She felt there was something wrong with her. She was ready to end the relationship with her new partner so she could have the time she needed to be alone. She did not understand that she could ask in a loving way for what she needed, and that her partner might actually want to give it to her. When she finally was able to tell him of her great need, he gave her a big hug and said it would make him happy to grant her that wish. He then added that he also needed time to himself, and did not know how to bring it up to her for fear of hurting her. They left the retreat a much closer and committed couple.

I'm so appreciative of all the ways that Barry honors my need to be alone. He accepts this need as a beautiful part of me and does not mind going out of his way to make sure my need is met. As a result, I have so much more love to give him after being alone.

Find Out What's Important to Her

BARRY LOVES ME BY DOING SIMPLE THINGS THAT
ARE REALLY IMPORTANT TO ME, AND NOT NECESSARILY
TO HIM. The big Christmas tree each December is one of
those things. Barry was raised in a traditional Jewish family
... without a Christmas tree. Christmas trees were important to our family. When my father lost his job, and
money was scarce, my parents told my teenage brother and
me that we would not be getting any presents under the
tree. We could each pick out a winter coat, which we badly
needed growing up in Buffalo, New York, but that would
be the only present. My brother had a job selling furniture
after school and I had babysitting jobs. My parents, brother,
and I pooled our money and got a Christmas tree. Though
there were no extra presents, we enjoyed the tree itself all
the more. As soon as the calendar turns to December, I start
thinking about our tree for that year.

Now, Barry could just tolerate the whole tree thing and
let me handle it all, but he knows how much it means to
me. He even grows the trees on our land, trims them all
year so that they will be just right, and then cuts them, leaving lower branches to produce a new tree. That way, each
tree just gets a major pruning. It doesn't have to die.

Then there is the grand procession to bring the tree
into the living room, setting it in the stand, tying it to the

wall (yes, one year it fell over two times while fully deco-rated), and then finally the trimming part. I know that Barry could easily skip a year without a tree, or maybe even skip it forever. It's a lot of work and gets messy toward the end. Sometimes it is the middle of January before I agree to take it down. On the way out of the house, the tree leaves a trail of thousands of dried needles. But this is a way that he loves me.

It's also important to me to have the kitchen clean be-fore we go to sleep. My Swedish mother once advised me to always do the dishes before I go to sleep, so I don't start the new day with yesterday's dirty dishes. I took her words to heart, and cannot go to sleep until the kitchen is all tidy. Sometimes we are so tired after working all day, Barry looks at the mess in the kitchen and sighs. I know he could easily go to sleep and deal with it in the morning, but he looks at me and knows how I feel without even talking about it. As tired as we are, we tackle the kitchen together and, by the end, we both have a good feeling about it. And each morning it is nice to start the day with a clean, orga-nized kitchen.

I also have the same feeling about our bedroom. I want the bedroom to be neat with all the clothes put away. Again, I know that Barry could easily be at peace with put-ting his clothes away once a week. But I feel our bedroom is a sacred place where we sleep, make love, and I say my prayers in the morning. I feel much better when it is kept neat. Barry's office, supply closets, and the garage are another matter. I try not to look, and only once a year insist on bringing a little order to those areas.

Sometimes I think it must be so hard to live with my idiosyncrasies. I can't sleep unless the window is open. Even on cold nights, when the temperatures in Santa Cruz fall below thirty degrees, I still crank open the window. Barry occasionally sighs from his side of the bed away from the window, but also realizes it's non-negotiable. I crave fresh air.

If Barry books a hotel for us, he knows to ask if the room has windows that can be opened. Some hotels don't, so he goes on to the next hotel on the list.

Once we were working in Canada in the winter and the temperatures were below zero. When we were getting ready for bed, Barry looked at me with pleading eyes. "Only a little bit," was my reply. Though the window was only open a fraction of an inch, I still had my fresh air. Most other people that night slept with the heat on and their windows closed. Barry tolerates this because he knows how important it is to me. It's worth it to him to pile on more blankets knowing how much the fresh air means to me. His sacrifice feels so loving to me.

Some years ago, I had major surgery on an afternoon. At 9:00 p.m. my husband came to me to say he was leaving to pick up my daughter and he'd be back after taking her to school in the morning. All I could do was say, "no,no,no,no,no." Although I could not articulate it, I was afraid to be alone in the hospital. He got busy on the phone making arrangements for my daughter's care for the night. He spent the night sitting up in an uncomfortable chair, fitfully sleeping and hugging a pillow. He was wearing a bright red Hawaiian print shirt. Every time I woke up, through the discomfort and drug haze, my eyes would be drawn to the bright red shirt and I would see my husband sitting there, hunched over and hugging that pillow ... and I felt safe. Afterwards, he told me he wore the shirt so I would be able to find him no matter how drugged up I was. That's how to really love a woman.

– CarolLee Cotter, Vancouver, WA

I know a woman who is a veterinarian and dearly loves animals. Her husband doesn't particularly like pets and doesn't really enjoy them in the house. But this woman loves her two dogs so much that her husband goes along with the dogs in the house. He has put his foot down to having them sleep in the bed though.

I know a man who married a woman who is very close to her sister. Every single holiday the woman wants to be with her sister and her sister's husband and five children. This man surrendered. He realized that the relationship his wife has with her sister is so important to her that he is supportive of it. Every once in a while, he asks to go on a vacation with his wife alone, and she will go along with it even though she would rather have her sister's family there as well. Sometimes this man jokes, "I thought I was marrying one woman when in fact I married a whole big family." He is good-natured about it because it is so important to his wife.

I enjoy how Barry loves me in these simple ways. We need to travel a lot for our work and so we sleep in different places frequently. At home we each have our favorite side of the bed. (Yes, you guessed it. I have the side closest to the window.) We have gotten used to our own sides. However, when we travel, my side might be up against the wall, while his side is by the window. Without even talking about it, he'll lie down on the side closest to the wall and give me the window side. There is something about that simple gesture, done in silence and without complaint, that translates to me, "Joyce, I love you and I'm willing to sleep away from the window so you will be more comfortable."

> *I feel loved by Jerry when he not only replaces a*
> *toilet paper roll,*
> *but he puts it on in the direction I prefer.*
> –Janis, Columbia, MD

Money and Loving a Woman

ॐ

THE BEATLES SING, "CAN'T BUY ME LOVE…" No amount of money can buy a woman's love, or prove your love for her. Money may bring her security, or comfort, but never love. And sometimes the more security and comfort, the less she actually feels loved. The reason for this is quite simple. A money differential is no different from a power differential. If you take care of her with your money, you are the "sugar-daddy." You're the father relating to her as a child. You have effectively taken away her power, and eventually her self-respect.

If You are the Breadwinner

The secret to a happy relationship is a balanced relationship. If you are the breadwinner, allow her to take care of you just as much in other ways. When our children were small, I brought in more of the money than Joyce. I have to admit, it was sometimes tempting to view the money as my money. This definitely was not healthy. Joyce could use the same argument: the children could be seen as more hers than mine because she spent more time nurturing them. I learned to view the money as one way I supported the family unit, and the children as one way Joyce supported the family unit. Then we were both supporting the family unit as a balanced couple. Joyce was taking care of me just as much as I was taking care of her.

If you are the one in charge of family finances, if you make more money than she does, and you feel she spends too much money, you may be tempted to judge and mistrust her. You may even try to control her. This never works. You end up not trusting her. You end up separate. There is a better way. It involves asking *vulnerably* for her help in managing your family finances. The key word is "vulnerably." If you demand her help the way a controlling father might of a daughter, you push her away ... you push love away. If you ask humbly and sincerely, accepting deep down that you really need her wisdom and strengths as a woman, you will get the help you need. I have found that Joyce has great wisdom in managing money, a kind of wisdom that I don't have. She has no idea how to even turn on Quicken on the computer, but she carries an overview of our finances that greatly helps me. Since I have been asking Joyce for her help, rather than trying to manage our finances entirely on my own, we have been doing much better financially.

If you make the money, and she focuses most of her energy on the children, you may be tempted to hide money decisions from her. This was true of Ray. He knew Kerry wasn't interested in their financial decisions and problems. He felt she had enough on her plate with the children and the household chores while he worked long hours each day away from home. He felt he was, in a way, protecting her by making all the financial decisions. Unfortunately, he made some bad decisions with his business that cost him many thousands of dollars. Rather than go to Kerry for comfort or help, he got a second mortgage on their home and put all the money back into his then-failing business. In a matter of months, he lost everything. And then it was more his shame than any noble feeling of protection that kept him from telling his wife.

One day, Kerry got a call informing her that their home was going into foreclosure. She felt blindsided. She also felt betrayed by Ray. She was so angry, she asked Ray to move out. Their eventual divorce might have been prevented if Ray had simply involved Kerry in every major financial decision.

If you are the breadwinner of the family, you love her by appreciating everything she does to take care of you. Society does not often place a monetary value on childrearing, homemaking, or emotional support. Notice everything she does during the day while you are at work: what she does for the children, how she takes care of the house, or the food she prepares. Also notice and acknowledge the non-physical ways she loves and cares for you: the ways she considers you in her decisions, the way she smiles at you, or her interest in your work or life. Especially notice her financial contributions, even if they are small: making handmade gifts instead of buying them, suggesting ways to save money, or taking charge of paying the bills. This will empower her, and you will, of course, benefit from this as a recipient of her love.

If She is the Breadwinner

What if she is the breadwinner of the family? Because of our upbringing in a money-oriented society, we may carry a bigger share of guilt about providing less money to the family than she does. This guilt may keep us from appreciating her financial provision, but she feels loved when we notice and acknowledge this contribution.

During a counseling session with a man who felt disgraced by his lack of ability to "provide" for his family, I realized the word "provide" comes from "pro" (support) and "vida" (life). I told him he "supported life" in his family more by his attitude than by making more money, more by his love of them than by his working for them. Learn the deeper meaning of the word "provide" if you want to truly love a woman.

To Resolve Conflict with a Woman

ARGUMENTS HAPPEN. We may wish we could get to a point in our relationships where we didn't need to ever argue but, as long as we have egos, we are immersed in the human condition, along with the attachment to our own ideas and desires. And that results in anger and all of our emotions. Yet anger does not have to be a horrible thing. In fact, we are blessed when we open to the lessons anger has to teach us, like more acceptance of all our human feelings.

Many people share that anger is the hardest part of their relationship, and often ask us for constructive ways to work with anger when it comes up. It's important to understand the nature of anger, as well as its purpose and usefulness. Most often, anger is a way we protect ourselves from the rawness of pain or fear — feelings that can become unbearable to our sometimes fragile and naked psyches. It is also a way we stand up for ourselves, rather than letting ourselves be controlled by another.

Irritation versus Anger

First, we need to distinguish between irritation and anger. There is a big difference between the little annoyances that are inevitable in relating and the more serious anger that arises from deeper issues. If something we do annoys her, like leaving our dirty socks on the floor, we need to ask ourselves how important it is for us to continue this behavior. Perhaps it's something we can let go of for the sake of harmony, and as a way to compromise with our beloved.

In addition, we need to be willing to resolve these little frustrations, to see them through to the end, to sincerely apologize when it is clear that one of our actions upsets our partner. It's just as important to communicate our own upset at something our partner did or said. And it's always best to have these communications in the moment, rather than waiting for a better time. Otherwise, these little upsets become buried in the soil of our being, only to explode out of us later. Also, if you wait to voice your annoyance until the sixth time your partner does that certain irritating thing, you carry the annoyance of the other five times in your voice, and your partner feels blindsided.

Going Deeper

When anger reaches a certain level of intensity, we need to understand that deeper issues may be crying out for attention. This higher amplitude of anger usually relates back to hurts older than the relationship, but triggered by the present situation. Harold, during a workshop, became angry at his wife because she left to go to the bathroom without telling him. His reaction was simply out of proportion to the offense. On deeper questioning, he shared that he felt abandoned by his wife. When asked if he had felt abandoned by anyone else, he revealed a profound abandonment by his mother, who left him when he was six years old. For Harold, his wife's action triggered the same feelings caused by his mother's abandonment.

Anger is not only an attack, it is most often a defense against hurt. It's difficult to not take it personally when our partner gets angry at us. It feels like we are being attacked or blamed, but this is often not the case. The anger is actually just a way this person is covering up their hurt or pain. Their anger is a sign that they are hurting. It is essential to remember this.

Anger, therefore, is also a cry for help. One of the highest things Joyce and I do in our own relationship is to recognize this truth. When one of us gets angry, the other tries to remember this is a call for help and tries to listen as openly as possible. When we're angry, we need and long for acceptance of our feelings. Joyce has told me she needs me to hold her when she is upset, even though it appears she is attacking me. This is not easy for me and requires some of the deepest courage I can muster. In fact, I can give support to angry strangers and friends far more easily than I can to Joyce. With Joyce, because of my attachment to her, I tend to immediately react to her anger at me as a personal offense. Still, I have on a few occasions immediately reached out and held her in my arms even though she was angry at me. This has helped her to let go of the anger and access the pain underneath. Other times, Joyce has been able to reach through my anger at her and hold me. We each need this connection just as much. Often, we are not successful at this method in the early stages of anger and get locked into defensiveness, which escalates the anger. But our goal is to eventually provide a safe place for the other's upset feelings.

Remembering that anger is a call for help allows us to be defenseless, and ironically, in defenselessness lies our real strength and courage. When we forget that anger is a call for help, we instead feel attacked and become defensive in an effort to protect ourselves. But as we more and more understand that someone who is angry is someone who is hurting, we can respond with more love. The proverbial lion with the thorn in its paw roars with pain and rage. You could feel defensive and assume the lion is angry at you. After all, this wild beast is loudly roaring and facing your direction. Or you could understand the roaring has nothing to do with you. The animal is simply in pain, and you can gently reassure it while you remove the thorn.

Any buildup of energy needs to be released, vented or transformed in some way. Anger is no different. Sometimes it just needs to be expressed as a release of steam, and we then feel better — and can perhaps subsequently access our deeper feelings of hurt or fear. We must remember, however, that anger does not need to be directed at our partner to be released. It can be effectively expressed by ourselves — for example, by yelling in a car with the windows closed or beating on pillows. It is important that we not ignore or distract ourselves from this energy. Sometimes, simply expressing anger in self-describing words ("I'm feeling angry right now") is helpful. Other times, it doesn't need to be expressed outwardly. It can be enough to feel (and accept that you feel) angry as another way to accept your humanity. Writing in your journal can be a helpful tool, as can physical exercise or being out in nature.

Ultimately, if we want to grow as a human being, we need to take full responsibility for our own anger and what is behind it. It is up to each one of us to accept and confront the hurt, pain or fear hiding underneath our anger. To maintain an angry stance is self-defeating, because it continues to cloak our deeper, more vulnerable feelings.

One of the ways we can prevent angry feelings is by taking better care of ourselves. Anger is most often a cry for help from within. Our inner child needs love and acceptance from ourselves most of all. When we forget this and only try to get it from our partner or from anyone else, we can become frustrated, disappointed — and angry.

How to Effectively Argue with a Woman?

And even more importantly, can the way we argue actually show a woman our love and respect? Joyce and I say yes. There is healthy and unhealthy anger. Here is an example of unhealthy anger:

Leonard was yelling at his wife, "Damn it, Mary, when are you going to give me any respect. I work all day long and come home to a messy house and dinner isn't even started. What do you do all day?!"

Mary was clearly intimidated. She was sitting wordlessly on the couch while he stood threateningly above her, clenching his fists as if he would hit her. She was hugging herself in a desperate attempt at self-protection, while the tears gave away her fear and pain.

No question here. This is obviously abusive and unhealthy anger.

Expressing anger is rarely enjoyable to your partner, but it can still be healthy and safe. I remember going through a phase in our early relationship where I felt expressing anger was definitely not healthy or safe. Joyce would *express* her anger and I would *repress* my anger, and even put her down for getting angry. Because that didn't work for her, her anger would then escalate to the next higher level. This would feel intolerable to me, and I would leave, regardless of where we were. Definitely not healthy on my part!

One day, we were in our small apartment in Los Angeles, and Joyce was expressing anger at me. I couldn't hold it in any longer. I yelled at her in anger. First there was a look of shock on her face, then gradually a smile appeared and she reached out and hugged me. She was actually thanking me for my anger.

I have stopped holding in my anger. Sometimes I go to the other extreme and let it out too loudly. At those times I imagine Joyce wishes I would go back to the way I was. But she assures me she would rather have me yell too loudly than not at all.

The Deeper Feelings under the Anger

Ideally, most anger can be headed off by addressing the feelings underneath, which are usually hurt or fear. When these deeper feelings are expressed and acknowledged, there is often no need for anger. For example, it is unavoidable for Joyce to sometimes say or do something that triggers hurt feelings in me. Usually this is completely unintentional. My goal is to say something like, "I trust you didn't mean to hurt me by saying/doing _____, and it did hurt me." When I make that statement to Joyce, it acknowledges that her intention was not to hurt me. It shows my love and belief in her. It also allows her to more easily hear my hurt and immediately apologize, which can quickly bring us back to love.

I remember some years ago when Joyce had fallen and broken her leg. We were traveling and I was doing all I could to make things easier for her. But one time, I left the toilet seat up and, when she entered the bathroom with her crutches, she criticized me for my lack of consideration. I was able to communicate my hurt and how hard I was trying. She immediately apologized and also appreciated all my efforts. She also realized the deeper frustration about her physical situation was being misdirected toward me.

I admit, expressing my hurt is more difficult for me because, like many men, I tend to not pay close attention to my hurt feelings. For lots of men, growing up as boys meant often hiding our vulnerability. Showing a bully that you were hurt was a no-no. It identified you as an easier target.

But what helps you to survive during your childhood doesn't necessarily work in an intimate relationship. Hiding your hurt feelings is one of them. If your loved one says or does something that doesn't feel good, and you ignore it, or rationalize that it wasn't meant to offend you, and you don't say anything, then you are not being honest with your feelings. If you do this often, you will pay too big a price. You will shut down your emotional availability even more. And you will shut your heart to your loved one.

Here's another example: Doreen had a long list of complaints about Brett, the many things he said and did that hurt her. Brett couldn't think of a single way Doreen hurt him. He needed lots of coaching from us to finally come up with one thing. Often, when he came home from work, and Doreen was busy with the children, it hurt him that she didn't acknowledge his presence or greet him. He felt her enthusiasm was entirely directed at the children, and not him.

Doreen was amazed that Brett actually felt hurt by this. He had never told her before. But she was quick to apologize. She simply wasn't aware that something she did was causing pain to her husband.

So men, pay closer attention to your feelings. Catch the sometimes elusive hurt feelings before they quickly go underground, then express them as a way to more completely love her.

Healthy Expression of Anger

When the hurt or fear is not felt and expressed, anger can be the result. Just to be clear, here are some guidelines for the healthy expression of anger:

"I" statements are rarely abusive. "I'm angry," rather than "You did _____," or "Why did you do _____."

Healthy anger is not intimidating or controlling. Even "I" statements can be abusive if you are scaring the person you are addressing. If you are physically or emotionally dominating this person, you are being abusive like Leonard. This includes not letting her speak or respond, and of course touching her in inappropriate or aggressive ways.

Healthy anger stays in the present, rather than bringing up unrelated things from the past to fortify your argument. "You came home an hour late without calling. Yesterday you forgot to bring out the garbage, and the day before you left your dirty dishes on the table." Not healthy.

Healthy anger does not generalize: "You're always breaking your commitments." Avoid the words "always" and "never."

Healthy anger does not make threats of any kind: "Break one more commitment and I'm out of here!"

Name calling or swearing is unhealthy.

After the anger is expressed in a healthy way, then it's time for both of you to address the hurt or fear underneath the anger. It's time for each of you to take responsibility for your deeper feelings, and apologize for hurting the other, including the hurt caused by the anger itself.

Address the hurt or fear beneath the anger and there will usually be no need to express anger. Prevention is always more effective. But if the hurt or fear remains elusive, you have a conscious choice to express your anger in a healthy way. Follow the above guidelines and you can have an abuse-free interchange.

When Joyce and I are angry with each other, we may initially take a short time-out. This can sometimes be very helpful, if there is a clear agreement on the length of time apart. As I said before, in our early marriage, rather than express my anger, I would simply leave and Joyce would have no idea where I went or how long I was gone. If I left her with our small children who were naturally upset because of the energy between us, she often felt completely abandoned. My fear and denial about my own anger translated to her as simply not caring. Our time apart now during times of anger usually has a healthier goal, to get underneath the surface anger to the deeper feelings of hurt or fear.

Our goal during angry times, however, is to stay connected and work it through to the end. We know we are done when we can sincerely hug and kiss one another and even laugh at our behavior. Because of this, the flame of our love and commitment to one another has been allowed to burn brightly.

I have felt most loved when my partner has been willing to face his deepest shadow fears and rage – the ones that he is feeling toward me – to face them, communicate them and feel them all the way through. I've only had this in one relationship and, amazingly enough, not in my two marriages. And whaddya know, that's what broke up both marriages. Neither one of my mates was willing to go through the fire with me. Neither one was willing to go to counseling and do whatever it took to come back to love. Neither one was willing to feel his deepest negative emotions, projections, expectations, disappointments, resentments and, by facing these feelings, actually go to a new level of intimacy.
–Starla, Santa Cruz, CA

Specific Rules for Effectively Arguing with a Woman

Along with the above general pointers, here are some more specific guidelines when you find yourself in disharmony with a woman:

1. Never use your size to your advantage. If you are physically larger than she is, and try to overpower her by looming above her, you are just trying to scare her into submission. You may win the argument, but your bullying has cost you her respect and love.

2. Also, don't try to overpower her with loudness. An argument is not a contest, where volume of anger determines the winner. This is also a scare tactic that will make matters worse, not better.

3. Avoid any reference to her being too emotional. Joyce used to say to me, "Barry, if you want someone more rational, you should've married a man!" She was right, and her comment usually stopped me from further criticizing her emotionality. It's her emotional nature that balances me. She's not too emotional. She's just emotional enough. And sometimes I'm not emotional enough.

4. If she fires accusations or questions at you in rapid succession, do not attempt to rationally answer each one. It can easily become an interrogation where, no matter what you say, you lose. Instead, let her know how her accusa-

tions are hurting you. That's being authentically vulnerable. Tell her you need her to just speak about her own feelings.

5. When both of your emotions flare, you might feel a desperate need to flee. Don't! She will feel abandoned and the argument will be that much worse when you return, because there will be the abandonment on top of the original argument. As hard as it is, stay and keep letting her know how you feel. If you feel you just can't stay in the same room, like we shared above, tell her you're leaving AND tell her you'll be back as soon as you can.

6. And this is most important. As soon as you can, look for and admit to your responsibility in the argument. Your ego needs to be right. Your ego needs to find fault with her. Your ego will effectively keep love away from you. Choose your heart instead. Your heart will give you the courage. (Remember that "courage" comes from the French word for "heart.") If you really have no idea what your responsibility is, just ask her to tell you what hurt her. When she tells you, rather than justifying or defending yourself, simply apologize. Remember, you didn't intend to hurt her, but you did. That doesn't make you a bad person. You are a good person who simply said or did something that triggered her. When you can say these words from your heart, "I understand that my saying or doing _____ has hurt you, and I sincerely apologize," there is a high likelihood that the argument will be over.

To Really Believe in a Woman's Greatness

A WONDERFUL WAY TO LOVE YOUR WOMAN IS TO BELIEVE IN HER GREATNESS. By your belief and support you can inspire her to greater heights. Some men mistakenly believe that they can keep their woman in the relationship by withholding appreciation and, worse, pointing out her flaws. By fostering her low self-esteem, they reason she will feel that she can't be with any other man. The opposite, however, is true. The more he encourages and believes in her greatness, the happier she will become and the more she will truly want to stay with him.

When Barry was in his psychiatry residency program, I worked in the same department. I knew when he would be giving his group therapy sessions and I would slip away from my work for a few minutes each day to watch him from the observation room. I felt in awe of his group-leading ability. Secretly, I dreamed that I could do the same thing someday, but felt that I wasn't good enough.

One day, I shared my dream with Barry. He said, "Joyce, I'm convinced you would be incredible leading groups."

"No, Barry, I'm too shy and too introverted to lead any kind of group."

Barry gave me that look that told me he didn't buy it for a moment and then said, "You're wrong! It's your sensitivity and intuition that would help you the most." His confidence in me was wonderful, even if I didn't feel it myself.

We next traveled for several years and then settled in Santa Cruz, California, to begin a psychotherapy practice together. As long as we were working with just one or two people, I was fine. But the thought of working with groups still terrified me.

Shortly before our second daughter was born, we started writing our first book, *The Shared Heart*. I loved the whole process of writing and was excited to have the book published. I didn't anticipate, however, that the book would then put me in front of people. The first book signing was at our local Unity Church, and a long line of people stood waiting to have us sign the book. Barry, the extrovert, was delighted to hug each new person and then sign their book. I was so overwhelmed to be with so many people that I sneaked into the bathroom and hid for the remainder of the time.

That evening, I curled up next to Barry on the couch. "I'm sorry," I confessed, "that I couldn't face all those people at the church today. Maybe you could give the talks and book signings from now on."

He wasn't going to let me get away with this. "Joyce, I want you to know that I believe in you. You have too much to offer other people. I want you by my side. I need you at my side!"

The next day, our first invitation came for a talk at a large church in Seattle. In the following days and weeks, the invitations came faster than we could deal with them. Barry rejoiced at the news and I shrank into the bedroom. Barry followed me and held me in my fear, "I'm convinced you'll do a great job with this talk. I can see how much you'll be helping people."

I managed to put it all out of my mind until I was seated next to Barry on the flight to Seattle. The anxiety started to grow. But when we were delivered to the church, and we walked in to find over a hundred people waiting for us, I panicked. Seeing a dark sanctuary through an open door on the side of the room, I grabbed Barry and dragged him through the door. We found a quiet pew, sat down, held hands, and I prayed with all my heart for the strength and courage to go back out there. Barry offered a prayer as well.

When he finished, he offered some advice, "If all those people out there were little children, you'd have no problem addressing them. You're great with children. You're natural with them, because they're not a threat. So here's what you have to do. Just see all those people as what they might have looked like when they were little."

Barry's advice did the trick. With shaking knees and a quivering voice, I made it through that first talk with Barry holding my hand. It took a full three years or more before I felt comfortable in front of groups of people. Barry supported me and gave me positive feedback after each talk or workshop. Barry's belief in me gave birth to a dream that I wanted but feared. Now some of the happiest times in my life are sitting or standing beside Barry in the workshops or talks – teaching, sharing, and loving. Thanks to Barry's belief in me, I am able to do something I truly love. I will always be grateful for what he has helped bring out in me.

Supporting Her Dreams

Listen to the dreams of your partner and support her to make them a reality. A woman I know, Sally, got married to her high school sweetheart and soon after had her first baby. By the time she was twenty-four years old, she had four small children running around her home. Her husband, Jake, worked as a mechanic. Being a mechanic had been his dream. Jake had talked to Sally and learned that her dream had always been to go to college and become a teacher. On his own he talked with the local college about loans and decided that it was time for Sally to begin her dream. He approached the idea with her on her birthday. She was thrilled, telling him she thought about it every day, but wondered how she could study with four young children. Then with a big smile on his face he said, "Sally, as my present to you, I will watch the children when I get home from work if you need to study. I believe you will make a wonderful teacher, and that you will love to fulfill your dream of going to college. I want to support you in your dream."

Sally enrolled the next day. It took her twice as long as the average student due to parenting responsibilities, but when she graduated, a proud Jake and four teenage children were cheering her on. Sally received a job teaching Women's Studies at the local college. Her classes were so popular that Jake encouraged her to get her master's and then eventually her PhD. She eventually became the president of that college. Her husband, Jake, continued to work as a mechanic in his shop. He is so proud to boast to his customers that his wife is a PhD college president. Sally is totally devoted to Jake and so grateful to him for supporting her in her dream of education.

Another woman I know, Ellen, completed all of her education and had a successful psychotherapy practice. She had also been a talented dancer with a brilliant career. All of her career dreams had been fulfilled. The one dream of hers that was not fulfilled, however, was the dream of being a mother. Ellen's husband, Pete, also had a fulfilling career. He had been married before and had two grown children. For Pete, the thought of having another child was not appealing. Because Ellen had such a strong desire and dream to be a mother, he agreed to try with her to conceive a child. He figured he would allow it to be God's will if they had a child.

Eight painful years went by in which they would conceive a child and then lose it in a miscarriage. After seven attempts, the doctor finally told Ellen that it was unsafe for her to try anymore. Pete was at peace. He had enjoyed raising his two children, and Ellen and he had a great relationship with them at that point. He was ready to put the idea of another child completely at rest. Ellen was not at peace. Her dream of becoming a mother was just too big to let it go. She approached Pete with the idea of adopting a child from China. Pete wasn't happy. The adoption procedure was long and expensive and he knew it would take him away from the work he wanted to focus on.

He sat with the idea for about six months. Ellen didn't bring it up again. We saw Pete from time to time during this period and we'd ask about the idea of adopting a child. We could tell from the expression on his face that he didn't really want to. On their anniversary Pete surprised Ellen with a card that had a little Chinese girl on the front. On the inside the card read, "Honey, your dream is important to me. Let's go and get our baby."

Two years later, after many meetings and hundreds of hours of paperwork and a long trip to China, Ellen and Pete came off the plane with a bundle of love in their arms. Their baby was and is totally precious. Ellen is thrilled to be a mother and is great at her new responsibility. And this darling little girl has Pete wrapped around her finger. One has only to glance at Pete's expression when his daughter runs into his arms, to know that he is also benefiting from helping Ellen fulfill her dream.

Believing in the greatness and dreams of your partner is a powerful way that a man can love a woman. By bringing out the best in her, you are supporting her to be all that she can be. Even if she then goes on to surpass you in education like Sally and Jake, she will be so grateful for your role in her development. You will always be her hero and her gratitude will be rich and deep. In her eyes you will be the wise one to be honored and adored, because you helped to unlock the key to her greatness.

When we took our children on a trip to Spain, we went to a flamenco dancing show. Our 8-year-old boy really wanted to see the next show that started at midnight. We had 3 other children who did not want to stay. Charlie & I loved to dance, so he loved the show as much as I did. But he insisted on staying with the children at the hotel while I got to attend the next show with our son. He would do this sort of thing often, taking care that I was enjoying life as he did.

When we moved from a city to a small town, I began noticing how the education in the schools could be improved. Charlie said, "If you really want to do something about this you should run for the Board of Education." So I did. Since we were new to town, we didn't know many folks, so we campaigned. Charlie volunteered to take one of the boys and knock on doors on my behalf. He did not just encourage me, he spent time following up with support.

–Joan Westgate, St. Helena, CA

To Really Encourage a Woman's Creativity

🧍

I SAW A PBS SPECIAL CALLED, MAKERS: WOMEN WHO HAVE MADE AMERICA. This three-hour documentary followed the rise of the women's movement during the years 1960-1980. It's hard to believe that women up until the sixties used to just be at home, watching the children, cooking all the meals and cleaning up from those meals, as well as doing all of the housework and errands. The woman was not supposed to have creative outlets, except domestic ones like sewing and cooking. The man was the head of the house, and many women felt just a little better than slaves to him. Thank goodness for the women's movement and the development of equal rights for women. Women are now encouraged in their creativity.

I will be forever grateful for the way Barry encouraged my creativity in the writing of our sixth book, *A Mother's Final Gift*. We were right in the middle of writing the book you are now reading when my mother went through her nine-month dying process. Barry and I and our three children, ages 30, 24, and 17, were the main support and "nurse aides" for my mother. My mother's dying process had such a profound impact on all of us, for she was truly excited about her "last adventure" on this earth … death. She was convinced that her creator cared about her so much that her dying process would be beautiful. For the three weeks before she died, she was as much a part of the world into which she was going as she was of this world. She was able to communicate all that she was seeing and hearing about the "heaven world."

After my mother died, I felt compelled to write a book about all that we had learned caring for her. I wrote most of the book myself, but also encouraged Barry and our children to contribute as well. I could hardly stop myself from writing, the drive to finish the book was so strong. Barry continued working on this book. Though he encouraged me in my writing, I could tell that he missed my enthusiasm for this book. I simply had no room in my heart for anything other than the book about my mother. And he understood this and encouraged me to pursue what was so strong in my heart.

After the book was finished, I was able to get a good agent in New York. Through her help, the book was looked at by all of the major publishing companies. One reputable publishing house was interested and the senior editor was all set to sign on the book. Then the marketing department shot down the idea, convinced that a book about dying would not be profitable enough.

I was crushed and cried a good part of that day. I had the fear that if this editor, who was so excited to publish the book, could not convince her marketing team, then no other editor would be able to do so either. At the end of a painful day for me, Barry held me in his arms and said, "Though it's a tremendous amount of work for me and I'll have to put aside our other project for now, we can self-publish your book."

This was a big sacrifice for Barry. For the next year, when we were not doing our regular work, Barry edited *A Mother's Final Gift*. As our ten volunteer editors submitted their ideas and changes, he incorporated them. He formatted the book, picked out the paper, as well as actively helping with the cover design. He put aside his own creative project to help me with my project.

A Mother's Final Gift has not brought a financial fortune into our lives, but it has gone on to help many people from the ages of fifteen to ninety-five. One woman has written to us that she feels it should be "required reading" for all people. From the many grateful letters we have been receiving, I feel fulfilled in knowing that writing and self-publishing the book was a worthwhile and essential project.

As soon as the book was published and on its way into people's homes, I again resumed my writing on our joint project with even more passion than I had in the beginning. For now I had the added gift of how much Barry was willing to sacrifice to help me fulfill my creative dream.

Sue Monk Kidd is the author of the famous book, *The Secret Life of Bees*, which went on to become a movie. She wasn't always a famous author. I knew her through *Guidepost Magazine* when she would occasionally write about being a homemaker, raising her two children, and being a loving support to her husband, a minister who loved his job. She supported him in every way with his creativity and his job. When the children were grown, she decided to write her first novel. During the year of writing, her husband, in his free time, then supported her by quietly making and bringing her lovingly prepared meals when she was too busy to sit with him. He also read over her writing and helped her with the initial editing. He gave up vacations so she could focus on her writing.

When the novel took off, suddenly she was being asked to speak all over the United States. Her publisher set up a speaking tour that would keep her away from home for months at a time. Her husband decided to take a year-long sabbatical from his ministerial job so he could support his wife.

I, along with millions of others, truly loved her book. I went to her talk in Santa Cruz. In the Capitola Book Café, I sat and observed Sue talking about her book, and her husband sitting quietly in the front row intently watching his wife, and occasionally taking notes. He must have heard her talk one hundred times before, yet he sat there in adoration of every word she spoke.

During the question and answer portion of the talk, I urged her to consider compiling all of her writings from *Guideposts* into one book for her readers. No one in the room had heard of *Guideposts* and there was much excitement about reading her other writings. I noticed her husband making notes after I asked my question. One year later, the book I had requested was published.

After Sue completed her talk, her husband helped sell the books. He opened each one to the proper place, asked the person's name, then said to his wife, "Now this is Joyce. She wants you to sign her book." This went on for the many people waiting in line. I stayed just to watch this man and spoke with him afterwards. I complimented him on his support, and he said that it is an honor just to help his wife and be by her side. When the books were sold, he packed up everything, put it in the car, and escorted his wife out the door to the waiting vehicle. Even though he was a star in his own job, he allowed himself to take a back seat while supporting his wife.

There are many ways to encourage a woman's creativity. I love roses and have such a passion for them. I also love dahlias. I feel like an artist when I'm in my garden, only rather than painting with paints, I paint with flowers. Barry loves the flowers, but would never take the time to grow them himself. He likes growing vegetables and fruit trees. Still, because I love these roses and dahlias so much, he helps me with the things I cannot do myself. As I add new plants, he digs the holes. He also takes his truck to get a load of compost for the roses and helps me put it around each rose plant. He seems to be forever fixing the fence that keeps the deer from eating their favorite food...roses. He also sets up a complicated drip system for the dahlias each year. I appreciate his help so much and it makes me so happy to see him willingly helping me. I always tell him it is a great gift that he gives to me. Every Mother's Day, Barry gives me the gift of anything that I need done in my garden. Not only is this a great gift, but it is also an act of love.

To Really Love a Woman is to Love Her Children

A POWERFUL WAY TO LOVE A WOMAN IS TO LOVE HER CHILDREN, WHETHER THEY ARE ALSO YOURS OR NOT.

I will let you in on a secret. A mother is incredibly drawn to you when you reach out spontaneously and give loving attention to her baby or child. She feels that an important part of her is also being acknowledged.

I remember the first time that Barry and I became parents. We had been together for eleven years and I thought we loved each other in the highest way possible. I didn't think I could possibly love Barry any more. Then our first daughter, Rami, was born. Several days after her birth, we were sitting together in our living room. Barry gently picked up Rami and began dancing around the room with her, singing to her about how much he loved her and all the fun they would have together. I looked at Barry and felt that I had never loved him as much as I did in that moment. To me he was simply irresistible, and I just wanted to run over and throw my arms around him and tell him how much I loved him. Instead I just sat and watched and my heart opened more to him in that moment than it ever had before.

The key word in the last paragraph is spontaneously. It's a major turnoff for her when a mother has to beg or nag to get you to pay attention to your child. But it's a loving act toward her, not to mention the child, when you spontaneously give attention to your child.

When I was a child growing up in the fifties, my mother stayed at home with my brother and me, and my father worked away from home. He returned every day at 5:30pm and my mother usually had dinner waiting. My brother and I flew into my dad's arms. All during dinner he wanted to hear about our day. When we were done sharing, he made silly jokes and made us laugh. After dinner we all helped with the dishes and then it was "Daddy Time." My father understood that my mother had had all the fun during the day being with us, so he wanted his time. My brother and I both felt that my dad enjoyed this time with us as much as we did. I don't know how he did it, but he kept us both amused with different games until our bedtime. Then he insisted that he be the one to put us to sleep with stories and kisses. For three years I had him read the same book to me, *Chip Chip*, about a squirrel. For three years my dad read and reread that book as if it was his first time. My dad passed away many years ago, but the memory of how much he enjoyed "Daddy Time" is my favorite one. I brought a much worn, frayed copy of *Chip Chip* to show everyone during my memorial talk about him.

My mother and father were married for over sixty years. There were many ways that my father showed his love for my mother, but "Daddy Time" when we were little children was her favorite and most meaningful. It was during his time with us that she got to explore her creative side, write a few cards, call her sisters or just sit peacefully with a cup of tea and be alone with her thoughts. After we were asleep, she and my dad enjoyed several hours alone together. She felt rested and could more easily enjoy his company. Playing with us had helped to release the tensions from work, and my father could more readily enjoy my mother.

There's a young couple I know, Brad and Julie, who just had a baby boy. They both had worked as river and mountain guides and now Brad worked in a sporting goods store, selling outdoor equipment. He wanted to be outside more and felt jealous of Julie who got to stay home all day and take walks with their baby. Therefore, when he returned home from work, he refused to help around the house or with the baby. If it was still light, he would go off by himself in the woods. If it were dark, then he would sit in the living room and read the newspaper. As the baby grew, he wanted more and more of Brad's attention, but didn't get it. Brad wanted Julie to take care of the baby and get him to sleep quickly. After the baby was asleep, then Brad wanted to have sex with Julie. She felt absolutely no attraction for him, plus she was tired from watching the baby all day. The couple grew further and further apart. When they came to us, they were thinking of separating.

Brad's complaint was that Julie never wanted to have sex with him anymore and was too tired in the evening to even want to talk with him. Julie felt discouraged and sad that she seemed to be raising their son by herself. She said this took so much out of her that she didn't feel like giving anything to Brad. It became obvious to us that Brad needed to give their son more attention, and allow Julie some free time and rest.

Rather than taking walks in the woods by himself, Brad started coming home from work and immediately put the baby in the backpack to set off for an adventure. They were usually gone for an hour, time that Julie desperately needed to rest. During this walk, Brad began to bond with his son. He talked to him about all of the adventures they would have together, and the boy responded with giggles. Sometimes the walks and time away from home would stretch to two hours, as Brad was beginning to have a lot of fun with his son. By the time they returned, there was a smiling Julie greeting them both with open arms and an open heart. She had needed the space from the baby to re-charge and get back to herself. Brad meanwhile was having so much fun with his son that soon he wanted to read him stories and put him to sleep. To his delight, he often found Julie attracted to him when he emerged from putting the baby to sleep.

There's a wonderful children's book called *The Man Who Kept House*. Our children loved this book and we read it over and over to them. In this story, a man works in the fields while his wife tends to the home and baby. When he comes home, he wants to be waited on, for he believes he has been the only one working all day.

One day, the wife has heard this enough and says, "All right, tomorrow I will work in the fields and you will stay home and take care of the baby and house."

The man laughs and says, "That will seem like a vacation to me."

"We'll see!"

Morning comes and the wife goes off to work in the fields. The man keeps laughing to himself that at last she will find out how hard he works, while she sits around all day watching the children.

All day long things go hilariously wrong for this poor man and, just when you think nothing worse can happen to him, it does. The wife returns to total chaos. The man bows down before her and says he will never complain again about her job.

It's not easy to stay home and take care of children. A powerful way to love her is to honor her in her job of caring for the children, and to give her as many breaks as possible to be alone. "Daddy Time" is such a blessing for the relationship and certainly for the dear children who will treasure time with Dad.

This same idea applies to families in which both parents have to work away from home. Usually, even though the woman has worked as many hours at her job as the man, she is the one who has to care for the children. Her heart will open ever wider if you spontaneously share in this responsibility. In households where the man stays home and cares for the children while the mother works, the opposite is true. Then the woman must be careful to give the man time away from the children. This same principle applies to blended families, where there are children of the mother and children of the father.

In our family, Barry and I both worked while the children were growing up. I worked much less than Barry in the office and counseling practice. We both did the workshops and writing together. My main focus was always the children, and Barry took on the mundane office work, like scheduling and paying bills.

After dinner, before he headed back to the office, he would look at our children and announce, "Friendly Tiger!" They would jump up with excitement. Every night, the "Friendly Tiger" (Barry) would roam through our living room causing little children to squeal with laughter and delight. This friendly tiger always did different and interesting things, making this game a highlight of the day. It was obvious that our children loved him very much. I would sometimes watch from the couch and marvel at how creative this tiger could be. I loved Barry so much as he wandered around our living room, and thought to myself that I had truly married the most wonderful man in the world. Sometimes he sensed my loving him and would include me as "Mrs. Friendly Tiger." Then he would come over and give me a kiss. After Barry was thoroughly worn-out, he headed to the office while I read stories and put our children to sleep. Our children are grown now, and the friendly tiger has recently come out of retirement to play with our grandson. The memory that remains still touches my heart as a beautiful way that Barry showed love.

To Really Love a Woman is to Love Her Family

IF A WOMAN IS CLOSE TO HER FAMILY, YOU LOVE HER DEEPLY BY OPENING TO THEM. If it is too emotionally painful for her to be close to her family, which is the case for some women, then you love her by supporting her in those feelings. Reaching out to her estranged family behind her back may come across as a betrayal. If she asks for your help, that's a whole other matter. But if she loves her family and is close to them, or even if she has a desire to be close to them, you can really love her by finding ways to connect with her family.

Barry and I came from different types of families. My mother was Swedish, soft-spoken, a good listener, and interested in many things. My dad was German, and he loved making people laugh, but his greatest joy was being with children.

In my family, when someone talked, everyone else listened. There was respectful interest in whatever topic someone brought up. My parents were both early civil rights activists, when it was not a popular thing to be. My parents were dedicated to their Presbyterian church and went often. They often invited foreign students from the

University of Buffalo for meals. They wanted my brother and me to have an open attitude toward all people of different nationalities. Sunday dinners often included Chinese, African and Japanese students. They also had a best friend who was gay. Though my mother was an excellent cook, food was seldom talked about.

Barry came from a Brooklyn Jewish family. When I first visited his family at age eighteen, I was shocked to observe that everyone talked at the same time. It seemed to me that no one was listening to anyone. If someone really wanted to be heard during a meal, they simply spoke louder than everyone else. Soon, it seemed to me that everyone was speaking in loud voices, almost shouting. I felt intimidated. Barry seemed to not notice any of this and just sat quietly eating his meal. This was normal to him.

When I first met Barry's father, he did not ask me the traditional questions like, "Where does your family live? What is your major in college? Do you have brothers or sisters?" Instead, he came down the stairs, shook my hand and asked, "Do you know how to make tuna salad?"

I said, "Yes. My mother was a good cook and taught me from the time I was quite young."

He wanted to know how I made it. I told him what my mother had taught me.

He waved his hand dismissively and smiled, "You don't know how to make tuna salad." He then proceeded in the next half hour to explain how he made tuna salad, even demonstrating with an imaginary knife how he chopped up the celery.

That was my first contact and conversation with Barry's dad, and I have never forgotten it. His love for food seemed strange to me at first. His eccentricities were sometimes over the top, but I grew to love these qualities about him. His favorite thing to do was go to the grocery store each morning. He would wake up with a list in his head. The main subject of conversation during a meal was ... the next meal!!

At the time I met Barry, his parents lived in a Jewish world, with all of their friends and neighbors being Jewish. Besides his dad's preoccupation with food itself, the kinds of foods were also different. I'll never forget my horror when we sat down to lunch during that same first visit, and I watched Barry's dad take a piece of gefilte fish from the jar and slide it into his mouth. Then, with a glint in his eye, he lifted the jar to his lips and drank the slimy gel. "Ahhh," he said, putting down the jar, with the gel still clinging to his mustache, "that's the best part of all." He then offered a piece to me, which I politely refused.

Barry's mom had been a first grade teacher for twenty years when I first met her. She loved children very much, but she sometimes treated her grown children as part of her first grade. The first meal I had at their house, I was politely told that I must wash my hands first and not to forget to use soap and scrub carefully until they were "squeaky clean." Though surprising at first, this quality became endearing to me.

Both Barry and I came from loving families. But as you can see, they were different. It was shocking for Barry to sit at our family table and realize that, when he spoke, everyone else would listen to him. At first, it made him uncomfortable, but then he got used to it.

Even from the early age of eighteen, Barry knew that part of loving me was also loving my family. He couldn't change how they were, so he found a way to fit in, just as I needed to do with his family. I never did learn how to make tuna salad as precisely as Barry's dad. At first I was a little intimidated, then, a few years later, we became vegetarians. No, not because of the experience with Barry's dad.

My parents loved to play cards. They had a weekly penny poker group that would fill our home with laughter every Friday evening. My mother was also part of a bridge group. But their favorite game of all was pinochle. During every family gathering on my dad's side, when the dishes were cleared, out came the pinochle cards. There was much laughter and fun as the whole family would play. There was no choice if you grew up in my extended family but to learn to play pinochle. The children sat with an adult learning the game until, one day, they could play by themselves.

Barry had never even heard of pinochle. It's a complicated game, but he patiently learned until he was also invited into the large family game. He was patient when my dad outbid everyone almost every time. When my dad's family was not there, we played four-handed pinochle. Barry was partners with my mother and I was partners with my dad. Barry and I have never played cards by ourselves but, with my parents, we played every time we visited and sometimes every night of the visit. I doubt that playing cards would have been Barry's first choice for an evening's activity. But he did it because he knew it made me happy and was a lovely way to be with my parents. Year after year, Barry and my mother were pinochle partners and a special bonding developed between them. They almost always won because my dad was fond of bidding high no matter what hand he held.

When my mother was ninety, she could no longer concentrate to play pinochle. By then, she needed caring. As we wrote in our book, *A Mother's Final Gift*, our three children, and Barry and I, took care of her in her final year of life and through her dying process. In one of the chapters of this book, Barry wrote that through the daily care of changing diapers, bathing and dressing, he went from being a son-in-law to being a son. In part, all of those years of being her pinochle partner allowed such a beautiful relationship in her final time of life.

Barry also developed a relationship with my dad through working with wood. They spent quiet times together out in the workshop creating things for the children. When my father was taken by ambulance to the emergency room, Barry went with my mother and me to the hospital. My dad was eighty-two years old and was having trouble breathing. He was also crying a lot, which is something that he never did. The emergency room doctor on duty did a thorough evaluation and said there was nothing wrong with my dad, and we should take him home. Even though Barry hadn't done general medicine for years, he disagreed with the doctor, which is not something that doctors do with each other, especially a doctor whose training is far less than the other.

This doctor then gave the case over to another doctor. The second doctor also proceeded to do a thorough examination and took a few more expensive tests and pronounced him fine. He said my dad must have been upset, which made his breathing more labored and made him cry.

Again, Barry disagreed with the doctor. He asked if they would be willing to do a simple test: Monitor his father-in-law's blood oxygen level while he walked, before sending him home. Well, as a result of the drastic findings of that test, it was determined that my dad had a pulmonary embolism and was immediately rushed up to the Intensive Care Unit of the hospital. This condition is difficult to diagnose in an emergency room. One of the symptoms can be excessive crying, which was the tip-off to Barry, who knew my dad. If my father had been sent home, there is a great chance he would have died that night. Barry stepped outside the bounds for doctor-to-doctor relations and risked embarrassment to stand up for my father. I am forever grateful to Barry, for my dad lived seven more healthy years.

I appreciate so much that Barry took the time and interest to love my family and accept them for who they are. It is definitely a way that he showed his love for me.

To Really Love the Little Girl Inside the Woman

THANKS TO THE WOMEN'S MOVEMENT, MANY WOMEN TODAY ARE POWERFUL, SELF-RELIANT, AND ABLE TO TAKE CARE OF THEMSELVES. If anything, the pendulum has swung in the opposite direction. Some women are too strong, too independent, and this can be a problem in relationship. They can try to control their partners too much, or not show enough vulnerability or need for love.

To really love a woman is to also love the child within her, *even when she is unaware of that child.* No matter how strong a woman is, a part of her is a small child, just like a part of every man is a small child as well. No matter how confident a woman is, there is a part of her that needs reassurance. No matter how nurturing she is, she also needs nurturing. No matter how loving, she also needs love, tenderness, and protection.

Over the years, Joyce and I have observed all the different things the child within needs. It usually boils down to one thing: *safety.* Without safety, our inner child goes into hiding, just like the lack of safety in our childhoods caused us to hide away our vulnerability. If a little girl doesn't feel seen or heard by her caregivers, she will learn to hide her need for this. She will not feel safe needing acceptance or validation. If she feels inadequately protected from physical or emotional harm, she will be in a hurry to grow up, and will develop a tough exterior shell. If her caregivers rely too much on her strength, or need too much from her, she will learn to hide her own need for love. She will give up on her own needs. She will become outwardly strong and independent, not trusting that anyone else could really take care of her. She will not really be happy.

Take Kaitlyn for example. She complained about having to take care of three children, ages four, seven, and thirty-eight. The last "child" was her husband, Tomas. She wanted him to be more responsible with their two "real" children. When she was too exhausted to put them to bed, she asked Tomas for help. Instead of calming them down, he would get them so worked up, it would then take Kaitlyn an extra hour to settle them down. When she left him alone with the kids, she didn't trust him to feed them properly or keep them safe enough. In her own words, "Why does he have to be such a little child? I need him to be a father. I need his help with our children."

Tomas admitted his difficulty taking responsibility, and his tendency to just let Kaitlyn take over with the children's care since she was so much better at it. He also wished Kaitlyn would "lighten up." He described her as too responsible, too serious, too much like his mother.

Joyce and I knew exactly how to proceed with this couple. Kaitlyn didn't only need Tomas to be a better father for their children, she desperately needed him to father her own inner child as well. Tomas, on the other hand, was stuck relating to his wife as a mother figure, and was blind to the little girl needing his love.

We pointed this out, and were immediately met with Kaitlyn's resistance. "I'm aware of my inner child, but every time I ask Tomas to be more present with me, he can't do it. How can I trust him to father me when he keeps disappointing me?"

Joyce and I saw that Kaitlyn needed to be more vulnerable, rather than asking Tomas the way a mother would ask a son. He would understandably feel pressured and perhaps defensive. We also saw that Tomas was blind to the little girl inside his wife. If anything, he seemed cowed by the largeness of her motherhood.

We asked Kaitlyn to lean her head against Tomas's chest, like a little girl leaning into the strength and love of a compassionate father. Mumbling, "This is never going to work," she reluctantly did as we asked.

In her physically vulnerable condition we asked, "Did your father ever hold you like this?"

"Are you kidding? My father needed my love and help much more than I needed his. I was the one taking care of both my parents. They both were alcoholics and pretty much useless as parents."

"Ah," we said, "but every child needs to be taken care of. You're no exception. Can you remember a time in your childhood when you urgently needed your father's care? Maybe a time when you were scared?"

Kaitlyn was quiet for a moment while she thought. "Well, yeah," she finally said. "One evening when I was probably eight years old, I was playing upstairs and my fourteen-year-old cousin came into my room and started getting aggressive with me. He started reaching into my pants. I told him to stop, but he wouldn't. I somehow broke away and ran downstairs because I knew my father was home. I don't remember where my mother was. I found my father passed out on the couch. When I told him I was scared and needed his help, he didn't even open his eyes. He just told me to go away. I had to spend the rest of the evening hiding from my cousin."

Kaitlyn was crying. In that moment, she looked like a helpless and terrified eight-year-old girl.

We noticed Tomas's hands had started gently caressing Kaitlyn's head the moment she started crying, and asked him what he was feeling.

"I never heard that story. It makes me sad. I wish I could've been there to protect you, Katie."

We seized the opportunity for healing. "Tomas, imagine yourself in that house, walking into Kaitlyn's room and seeing her cousin molesting her. What would you like to say?"

Tomas seemed on fire, "Stop touching her this minute! How dare you take advantage of her like that! Leave this room immediately!"

The power coming through her husband caused something to let go inside Kaitlyn. It was just what she needed.

She started sobbing uncontrollably. After a while, she found her voice, "Nobody's ever protected me like that."

"Kaitlyn," we urged, "open your eyes and look at Tomas."

She did.

"Can you clearly see a father who is able to take care of you ... even protect you?"

"I never knew this part of you, Tomas," she meekly admitted. "I like it."

"And Tomas, can you clearly see that eight-year-old girl, still needing love and safety?"

Tomas smiled warmly with moist eyes looking down upon his wife/daughter's head against his chest, "Katie, I think I've never seen you so beautiful, so real ... so vulnerable."

Now both were beaming through their tears.

"Tomas and Kaitlyn," we began, "this is a key to your happiness as a couple. Positioning yourselves as often as possible just like this as a nurturing father and little girl can be one of the most powerful practices you could ever do together. The father in you, Tomas, has been dormant, and the little girl who needs safety in you, Kaitlyn, has also been in hiding, just like you had to do that night so long ago. Express these two parts of yourselves, and your marriage will come back into balance, and you will soar together into a much higher love than you ever thought possible."

I have had hard pregnancies and this one, my
third, has been the worst by far. I get very emo-
tional and I can cry or get nuclear angry in a
moment. These emotions flow through me and I
have taken to just flowing along with them and
exploding daily in one way or another. Believe
me when I say, I have not been fun to live with.
After a rare moment of intimacy with my hus-
band Milton, we cuddled on the bed and he
gazed lovingly at me and said "I love you."
I asked, "How could you say that? I have been
horrible and bitchy and I have been picking at
you constantly. How could you lie there and
say that with love and adoration for me in your
eyes?"
He cuddled me close, his voice full of emotion
and said, "Because I love all of you, every part
of you and I accept you for who you really are."
–Barbara Rivera, Woodbridge, NJ

Joyce: A woman needs to know that her beloved can
be there fully for her when she most needs him. She needs
to know that the loving father presence within him can
come to the surface in a strong, powerful, and compassionate way when her need is the greatest.

In 1986, I was pregnant with our third child. Our first
two children were girls, and I had a strong sense that this
baby was also a girl. The name "Anjel" had come to me in

a dream. As with the other two pregnancies, I was very excited. I loved being a mother. Our two little girls, Rami and Mira, were ten and five years old and were excited to invite another little sister into our home. They thrilled to feel the baby move within me, and invented little ways to "play" with the baby. Barry was also excited and loved being a father. At six months of pregnancy, I sensed that I wasn't getting much bigger, but didn't pay much attention to this. I felt healthy and in tune with our baby.

Our nurse midwife came for a routine check-up and a worried look crossed her face. She suggested that I go to the hospital for an ultrasound. As Barry filled out the paperwork, I walked with Rami and Mira to the ultrasound room. I did not feel any apprehension since I felt so healthy. I was treated by the hospital staff without warmth. As Barry still had to be filling out papers, I was alone with Rami and Mira. A technician came, performed the ultrasound, and quickly left without a word.

Finally, Barry came and stood by my side and held my hand. The attending physician came in, roughly repeated the ultrasound and then, in a voice that felt accusing rather than sympathetic, said, "Your baby is dead." Then he took Barry by the arm and walked outside with him. He spent several minutes explaining what must be done for me, and then left.

Barry opened the door to find me crying with the girls. From that moment, he took full command of the situation. He comforted the three of us. The pain was so deep that I felt I was falling into a pit of despair. Barry let me cry. He sat with his arms around the three of us, until I was ready to leave. As we slowly and painfully walked out to the car, I felt his loving arms around me and somehow I knew I would make it through the pain. I felt safe to feel all of my feelings.

Barry arranged for our girls to be taken back to our home, then brought me to a compassionate obstetrician. A surgery was scheduled for the next day. Driving home from the hospital, Barry suggested that we stop at the beach. I stood at the water's edge and screamed long and loud, the waves of a mother's agony pouring out over the waves of the Pacific Ocean.

Because of the death of our baby, and the fact that I needed surgery and anesthesia, I felt very vulnerable. For several days following the news of the death, I needed Barry so much, and he was there for me. He was there with me when the milk came into my breasts, and there was no baby to nurse. He was there with me as we continued to support our girls in their grief. He was there with me at night when I would cry myself to sleep.

Barry: I don't think I've ever seen Joyce so vulnerable, so childlike, so needing my comforting. And it was precisely this vulnerability that drew out the father in me in the most powerful way. I felt extremely honored to father her, to be strong for her, to hold her firmly and securely in my arms. It was so obvious that she needed to be loved as a child, not as a woman. Yes, her grief and helplessness perhaps made it easier for me to father her at that time, but to really love her I needed to put my own needs on hold for that time period, especially my needs as a man to hold Joyce as a woman.

Joyce: After several days, I was strong enough to start healing on my own, and Barry went about his activities. But the fact remains that for those several days when I needed him the most, he was fully there for me. He gave me his full attention and love. I have not felt such a deep, urgent and extreme need for Barry since then, but that event has powerfully shaped my relationship with him. I know that in a time of crisis he will be there for me. I can trust that. That trust has allowed me to rest more fully in our relationship. All these years later, Barry's complete love and compassion continue to bless my life every day.

Barry: Joyce usually makes it easy to love her as a child. When she is having a difficult time, or is sad or over-whelmed, she will often approach me and ask in the vulnerable voice of a little girl, "Barry, could you please hold me and tell me everything will be all right?" Now, I may be busy at work, and not in the most loving or sensitive mood, but Joyce's vulnerability blasts open the door to my father-hood. Can you imagine being deeply involved in some project that had to be done in that moment, and your five-year-old daughter rushes into the room with tears streaming down her face? Would you say, "Not now, I'm busy?" I don't think so. You'd drop everything to hold and comfort her.

It's the same with the expression of true vulnerability. When Joyce reveals the fear and pain of her inner little girl, without the demanding energy of a woman or a mother, I feel empowered as a father. Her vulnerability opens my heart wide. All I want to do is hold her tenderly and securely. I feel no resistance.

To really love a woman, you must push past the demanding, or even angry, mother, and hold the hurt or scared little girl. This is a real test of unconditional love. When Joyce is angry at me, which can be unavoidable at times, I may see the hurt little girl showing through her eyes, but it can be extremely hard for me to stop being defensive. Every part of my ego wants me to protect myself from getting hurt by her anger. I feel attacked. I feel like a small boy who did something wrong ... again ... and is being scolded by his mother. It's my heart though, the loving father part of me, that still wants to comfort her.

I remember, in our earlier relationship, one of the first times my heart overpowered my ego in the face of Joyce's anger. Her voice was raised and sharp, and the words were coming at me like bullets, but I could clearly see the hurt little girl needing my love. The bullets changed into cotton puffs. I no longer needed my shield. My defensiveness fell away and I spoke directly to that hurt little girl. "Joyce, could I just hold you right now?"

For a moment she looked confused, for I had probably never made this kind of offer in the face of her anger. Then her face softened and she said yes. I pulled her into my arms and she relaxed against me. She had been angry because she was not feeling fathered by me. The sincere offer to hold her was exactly what she needed … a direct expression of fathering love.

One important reminder here: For too many couples, touch is equated with sex. There is not enough non-sexual touch, touch and holding that doesn't lead to sex. Many women have expressed their fear about letting their inner child be held in a vulnerable way by their partner. They fear that touching or holding will sexually arouse their partner, or will lead to the expectation of sex. So, they don't allow any touch. But everybody loses here. Instead, make clear your inner child's need for non-sexual touch, the sacred touch between a child and parent. Make time for this kind of holding in your relationship, and you will see that, other times, your sexual relationship will be even more fulfilling.

My husband Charlie knows that I am a fool for touch. I love to begin each morning by lingering together in bed. I call it "cuddling meditation." There is something very basic about this connection that reminds me of being a baby, being welcomed into the arms of my loving mother. The weight of responsibility that I normally carry is put down for a time, and I can rest into the strong arms of my beloved. I feel taken care of. There is nothing to do, nowhere to go, nothing that needs my attention in this moment.

–Linda Bloom, Santa Cruz, CA

Think of the woman you love. Can you visualize her face? Can you see past her adult face to her childlikeness?

If possible, get hold of a photo of her as a small child to use with this inner practice.

Imagine (or remember) what she looked like as a small child ... an older child ... a teenager.

Imagine (or remember) the suffering she endured while growing up, the lack of acceptance for her uniqueness, the rejection or abandonment, or the physical or emotional abuse.

Now, imagine comforting that child or adolescent, holding her with love and safety, holding her like you would your own small child.

Hold the woman you love the way a parent would hold a little girl.

Let her know she is safe. Don't expect anything from her in this moment ... especially sex. Encourage her to really let down her guard.

Give her permission to talk about and feel her fears, her pain, and her sadness.

Do not, I repeat, do not ... try to fix her. She's not broken. Put your toolbox away for now. Instead, just do two things:

Listen to her.

Let her know how beautiful she is, especially in her vulnerability and feelings. Speak to her as a loving parent, giving her the messages she most needed to hear as a child.

Making a Woman Laugh

I LOVE THAT JOYCE THINKS I'M FUNNY. I love to make her laugh. It is without a doubt a wonderful way I love her. For our third and fourth years of college, we lived in separate cities, Joyce in New York City and I in Boston. We thought it was right to separate, but our hearts kept bringing us back together. After a weekend of being together one time in Boston, Joyce got on the bus in tears. We were both sad to be parting. I started making funny faces looking up at the bus window, and she started laughing. There were a few other people on the bus who started laughing too.

I like to think that my humor has gotten a bit more refined over the years. I don't need to make faces to get Joyce to laugh. Sometimes, when she is having a hard time and needs to talk, a sprinkle of sensitive humor at the right moment is just what she needs to see a situation from a different angle.

Something else about humor: When I try too hard to be funny, I rarely succeed. When I'm invested in getting Joyce to laugh, it usually doesn't work. And please, never, ever think you're being funny when it's at someone else's expense, or putting down another person. It may work in the clubs, but it doesn't work with the one you love. Also, there can be a fine line between teasing and anger. Learn the difference. If you're even slightly annoyed at her, your teasing will carry a camouflaged version of that annoyance. And when anger, irritation, annoyance or frustration is hidden underneath attempted humor, it actually hurts more because the recipient is not prepared for what is really coming.

It also doesn't work to hide behind humor. We have seen more men than women use humor as a way to hide their feelings. In our counseling sessions or workshops, we sometimes see a real comedian who loves to make people laugh. It gives him great pleasure to make his woman laugh. In fact, it is her laugh that lets him know they're good as a couple. But this can become unbalanced. He needs to know they're good as a couple for deeper reasons.

If Joyce or I sense a comedian is using humor to cover up uncomfortable feelings, we will confront him. His partner probably will not be laughing. She can feel that he is hiding, and this is not funny to her.

Learn to be completely honest with your feelings, and your humor will really make her laugh. When you're not hiding behind your humor, you become a much funnier person.

After 20 years of marriage (by Barry and Joyce)
and more transformation than I would have
ever imagined, what means the most to me is
how Bob is simply there for me. Day in, day
out. Seeing me at my best and my worst.
Whether I'm predictable or surprising. Fun and
playful or down in the dumps and in need of his
diplomacy and wisdom. Cheering me on. Crack-
ing some cosmic joke just when I need to hear it
the most. Reminding me who I really am when
I forget.
Judyth Reichenberg-Ullman
Langley, WA

Playing with a Woman

Joyce and I often hear from both men and women, "We need to play more. We've gotten too serious." To really love a woman, you need to learn how to play with her.

Play can be structured or unstructured. Structured play can include sports, games, hiking, or ballroom dancing. You love her by finding out her favorite forms of structured play, and then making it happen as often as possible.

Many women also crave unstructured play, spontaneous moments of joyful connection. For many men, this is often synonymous with sex. There is nothing wrong with bringing more play into your lovemaking, especially if you can tell this is making her happy. However, if you start playing with her with the secret hope and desire for sex, she will often read between the lines, feel your motive, and may be turned off. This is because she wants to play with you in a more childlike way, which has nothing to do with sex.

Some women love physical play, including wrestling. Be careful here. You may be used to wrestling to win, rather than just play. If you get competitive, the play part goes out the window. You may be bigger than her. Never use this to your advantage. When you overpower her, it is certainly anything but play. Picking her up and throwing her into the water may work in high school, but it rarely works in marriage. Instead, learn how to be non-sexually physical with her. Just pretend the two of you are young children, making up games as you go.

Dancing can also be a form of unstructured play. Joyce and I love to dance. We may start out structured with dance moves we have previously learned. What we really like, however, is when we transition into unstructured play, like when I try to lead her in an experimental move, it bombs, and we end up cracking up with laughter. Or when we're alone in our living room, put on a sensual piece of music, and try to do the Argentine Tango. Except for one problem: I typically get sexually aroused and, like many men, can no longer pay attention to what my feet are doing. It then becomes a sexual moment (as we described earlier). If Joyce is still wanting to dance, it then becomes a comical moment, but only if I can let go of the sexual moment.

Unstructured play requires non-attachment. If you are attached to any particular outcome, it no longer is unstructured play. My letting go of the sexual moment allows us to have even more fun.

Teasing can be a beautiful form of play, but only if it is completely devoid of anger or judgment. Joyce was teased as a child because her sensitive emotional nature was not seen as acceptable. This teasing was traumatic for her. Somehow, over the last many years, I have learned to tease Joyce with love. I tease Joyce for her x-ray vision, her uncanny ability to see through situations, or the way her deep loving is next to impossible to resist. And how do I know there's no negativity in my teasing? Quite simple. She laughs in the most genuine, wholehearted way. I love to make her laugh. Her laughter is important feedback to me, letting me know I am successful as a lover!

Love Her in Public Too

IT'S NOT ENOUGH TO LOVE HER WHEN IT'S JUST THE TWO OF YOU. Don't ever hesitate to show your love in public as well. During our ballroom dancing classes, our instructor frequently urged us to show off our woman. "Your job," she would say to the leaders, "is to make her look good!"

Okay, it doesn't need to be overdone when you're in public, except on the dance floor. And if she's an introvert, you might embarrass her by gushing too much around other people. Just be sensitive to how she feels, just as much as how you feel.

The problem is usually on the other side, not enough public love and affection. Let's face it; most men receive strong indoctrination against showing love. It's a sign of weakness. Joyce and I recently watched the movie classic, *Grease*. John Travolta's character, Danny, and Olivia Newton-John's character, Sandy, had a summer love affair before their senior year in high school. Sandy had moved and was finishing in a new high school. It turned out to be Danny's school. They met with all his friends around. Danny was "Mister Cool" through and through, denying any connection with Sandy, which deeply hurt her.

I have to admit, I was a little like Danny when I was eighteen and newly in love with Joyce. I was embarrassed about showing love in public. I was sometimes even embarrassed about walking next to her. Once, we were walking down the hill from Hartwick College, which we were attending, into the town of Oneonta in upstate New York. Joyce had a childlike bounce to her step, completely uninhibited and unashamed. I asked her to walk more like an adult (that is, an adult in my mind!). She refused and told me I needed to accept her just as she was. My response was to cross the street and keep pace with her from the other side of the street. It would have been embarrassing if a friend happened to pass one of us and notice the other across the street. Sometimes I have to wonder why Joyce stayed with me!

Well, thankfully, I did change! I clearly remember a fraternity party the following year. Everyone seemed to be dancing. Then a slow dance began. I held Joyce close and we swayed to the music. It was perhaps the first time I truly let go of my image of how to act in public. I got lost in the music, the feel of Joyce's body so close to mine, the smell of her hair and skin. Together, we both got lost in an insulated bubble of love, neither of us caring about what anyone else on the dance floor thought. The problem was that we were alone on the dance floor. The moment the slow dance had started, person after person had left. By the end of the song, we were the only ones out there and, in the total silence, while all eyes were upon us, some curious, some incredulous, Joyce and I kept swaying in love, completely oblivious to the scene we were making. In that moment, in our insulated bubble of ecstasy, we inadvertently announced our love to the world!

So, how can you love her in public? Again, be sensitive to her feelings just as much as to your own. Reach out and take her hand because she likes it. If you take her hand because you like it, it may come across as sweet, but it is not necessarily demonstrating your love for her.

When with friends, put your arm around your beloved while talking with other people, especially another woman. Give a clear message to everyone about whom you're with and whom you love. Do this especially if she feels nervous or insecure, or you're with your friends rather than her friends.

Don't make the mistake of ignoring her in public, in the name of being independent or fearing codependence. Something else may be at play. Another woman giving you attention may be flattering to your ego. You might think, "What harm could a little innocent flirting do?" First of all, flirting is never innocent or harmless. Flirting is an exchange of sexual energy. It is degrading to her, and gives a clear message that you are not committed to her ... that she is not special to you.

So many times, men will say to us, "She is too jealous and insecure!" In other words, she has the problem. Or: "I'm not having sex with other women! Why does she get all bent out of shape?" Sensitive women tend to have radar for subliminal sexual energy exchanges, also known as "leaking sexual energy." You may feel you're having an innocent conversation with another woman, but if your woman feels hurt or abandoned, pay close attention. You may have something important to learn from her. If you feel it is hampering your style, or obstructing your freedom, to include her or put your arm around her, then you have a problem! It is also your problem if you feel that including her might somehow upset the other woman. You may have a fear of commitment, or a fear of attachment, which by the way, almost always boils down to your own fear of abandonment.

Love her by including her in your conversations. If she's deeply involved in her own conversation with someone else, don't drag her away. Instead, quietly approach and stand next to her, and perhaps ask to be included in her conversation. But if she's standing by herself, you love her by bringing her into your conversation.

Love her by experimenting with different ways of public shows of love and affection. Joyce and I are often in airports. We watch lovers being re-united after a flight. They throw themselves into each other's arms. Even though we travel together, we had the idea of pretending that only one of us had been traveling. Arriving in baggage claim, a common area of greeting, I might call out to Joyce, "Sweetie, how was your flight?" And then we fall into a lover's embrace, not ashamed to hold one another close and even passionately kiss as lovers who have been separated. It's something that is completely sanctioned in baggage claim. Even if it were not, people look at these two passionate seniors and think it's cute!

To Really Love the Woman Within

JOYCE AND I BOTH FEEL THAT OUR SOULS, THE ES-
SENTIAL PART OF US, ARE BOTH FEMININE AND MASCU-
LINE. The highest marriage, the most spiritual joining,
takes place within ourselves, not with an outer partner.
True, the relationship we have with another person can
mirror this inner relationship, and help point the way to
the real joining within us. Yet it is seductively easy to get
lost in the outer relationship and sometimes completely
miss the most important relationship. The illusion of relationship is that it only takes place outside of you. The truth
about relationship is that it mostly takes place within you.

To the extent you love your inner woman can you love
your outer woman. If you refuse to love your inner femaleness, you will try in vain to really love the woman in your
life. *If you right now are feeling resistant to this concept, this
chapter may be the most important chapter in this book.*

Projection is an often-subtle force in relationships. The
love we need from a woman is the love we have within us
already. It's just easier to see, or want, that love from our
female partner.

Does that mean we don't need the outer woman, that
we only have to receive what we need from our inner
woman? Some might say, "Why bother with outer relationships at all? It's just a distraction from the most important

work within. I can join a monastic order or just stay at home and meditate on my inner woman." Certainly, this is always an option, but we would say that the path of conscious relationship with a female partner can powerfully teach you about your inner woman. Loving the woman in your life can provide the fastest path to loving your inner woman. Accepting the femaleness you see and feel in your partner is a powerful way to accept your inner femaleness.

John, a man in his early thirties, was convinced his wife of four years, Linda, was more spiritually evolved than he was. This conviction kept him from trying to be with her in a spiritual way, so he avoided praying or meditating with her, reading spiritual books with her, or discussing spiritual matters with her. Because he lifted her onto a pedestal, high above himself, he saw her as out of reach, and they couldn't have a close relationship.

My work with John was to help him see that he was looking not only at Linda but also at a mirror reflection of himself. I encouraged him to look at, feel, and reclaim his own spiritual beauty. Part of each counseling session was spent in silence. I encouraged him to look into my eyes, to use me as a mirror to see his own higher self. It was new for him to do this, because he had never thought of himself as a spiritual person. Yet it was also refreshing — and eye-opening.

As he realized Linda was not above or ahead of him, she became more of a real person, within grasp, within relationship range. The more he was able to accept his own spiritual nature, the more he was able to love Linda as an equal partner.

At one of my annual men's retreats, the difficulty in understanding women became a central theme. One after another of the men shared his challenges with his female partner. During dinner on Saturday night, after a deep and vulnerable day for the men, I was feeling the need to give them a break for the evening – maybe do something lighter or more entertaining. Patrick and I came up with a funny skit. I would pretend to be his wife Judith (whom I actually knew), and he would try to understand and communicate with me. We came up with some pretty funny lines. Except we had no idea what was really in store for us!

The evening program began with several of the men sharing their musical talents. Then, I introduced my idea. I felt vulnerable, even though it was my intention to keep it light. It was still a risk for me. I found a feminine-looking scarf to put around my head and I was now a woman. Patrick and I ran through our semi-rehearsed skit, some of which was funny, and some of it more serious.

When we were done, another man raised his hand and asked his wife/me, "When we make love, why do you always need to be on top?" Many of the men laughed, thinking this was intended as a joke. I, instead, listened inside for my inner woman's voice and answered, "I need to feel more in control, not only during sex, but in my life in general." The man nodded with understanding. Women may need to be on top for other reasons, but the woman within me spoke knowingly to this particular man.

Then, without warning, the mood shifted with Tony's words to his wife, "I try so hard to protect you. I do so much to make sure you feel safe. Why are we not more connected?" He looked like he was on the verge of tears.

I instantly felt the answer and compassionately spoke, "You're so busy being the strong one in our marriage, you rarely give me a chance to protect you. If you would only come to me for help, or lean on my strength, it would make me so happy. We would then be so much closer."

Tony started crying and spoke, "I never realized that. I've been so vulnerable here at this men's retreat, but I don't show you this part of me. Thank you for helping me understand."

And so the mood shifted. My intentions of a light and whimsical evening went out the window.

Ron was the next to speak. "I see how afraid you are. I just don't know how to help you with your fears…"

I interrupted him, feeling what his wife would want most to say, "Dear Ron, rather than focus so much on my fears which, I admit, I maybe talk too much about, I need to hear about your fears."

Again, the message from the women (and the woman in me): stop attributing all the vulnerability to me. Be more vulnerable yourself. Rather than trying to fix me, which keeps me weak, let me help you, which makes me strong.

Ron got it. And I found myself getting more and more energized. I was really getting into this special kind of role-playing, which was turning out to be so much more than role-playing. Even though the mood in the group had turned serious, all the men were into it as well. Somehow Barry, the workshop leader and the man, had vanished. In his place was every man's special woman. Even the single men addressed questions to the significant partners from their past.

Burt needed to address a former lover. "We had so much trouble communicating. You would ask me a deep question. I would start to ponder the answer but, before I could even start to speak, you would ask me another question. This would drive me crazy, so I ended up wordless, and ultimately, woman-less."

Unlike Burt, I didn't have to ponder long for an answer. The woman in me spoke, "I, like many women, am so clued in to my feelings that they always seem to be on the surface, easily accessed. I should have given you more time to answer my feeling-oriented questions. I see now that it just took longer for you to get to your feelings. Each time I got impatient and asked another question, it drew you back up to your head and you had to start the process again. This was my part. Your part was not stopping me to give yourself the time. Instead, you just got more silent. Maybe we would still be together if we both understood this dynamic..."

Burt couldn't resist, "Barry, where were you when I needed you!"

What I "planned" to last perhaps fifteen minutes, ended up lasting one and a half hours. Every man in the room got to understand something important about a woman in his life. We ended with a little more music and then called it an evening … except I couldn't sleep. For the next few hours I was wide awake. I had activated my inner woman, my feminine side, and I actually had some difficulty getting back to my masculine side. It was exhilarating. I lay in bed deepening my understanding of Joyce, what she needed from me, especially my own vulnerability and the expression of my deeper feelings.

I wish every man could have my experience of such deep attunement with the inner woman. I believe it would so much help his relationships with women. In the end, I deeply believe, as souls, we are both male and female. Taking birth as one sex just seems to partially eclipse the expression of the other sex. For me, it just took the Saturday evening of a men's retreat to more deeply drive this point home.

Practice: Loving your Inner Woman

Sit or stand in front of a mirror. Look deeply into your own eyes. This takes time and practice. Most people find it difficult to do this. You might be tempted to give up after a brief try, but please don't. This simple practice can change your whole life.

Breathe deeply and slowly. Allow each conscious breath to take you deeper into your eyes, the windows of your soul, which is both masculine and feminine.

Concentrate on seeing your inner woman. There are qualities you attribute to women that you don't attribute to yourself. Find out what they are by looking deeply at your inner femaleness.

They may be positive qualities like sensitivity, nurturing, spirituality, gracefulness, ability to multitask, or the ease of expressing feelings. Your work is to see and accept all these "feminine" qualities in yourself. This will allow you to really love a woman.

They may be negative qualities like bossiness, inflexibility, too talkative, seriousness, lack of concentration, physical frailty, or needing too much. Yes, these too

230   VISSELL

are also within you. You really love a woman by accepting these qualities in you, rather than only projecting them onto her.

If you want to be a better lover, do not avoid the mirror. Use it more than only to shave, brush your hair, floss your teeth, or criticize the size of your belly. The mirror is a powerful tool for loving the woman in your life by loving the woman within you.

To See the Goddess

TO REALLY LOVE A WOMAN IS TO SEE THE DIVINE, ETERNAL BEING SHINING OUT FROM WITHIN HER. It's not enough to see her outer beauty, no matter how captivated you are by it. If you take the time to really look into her eyes, the windows of the soul, you will see a goddess, a vast, ageless, gorgeous expression of the divine feminine.

I will never forget the first time I saw the goddess in Joyce. It was 1972. We were twenty-six years old, sitting on top of a large boulder in the mountains outside of Los Angeles, where I was in medical school. We were recommitting after a painful separation. Perhaps the pain was needed to open both our hearts wide to something deeper than our bodies, minds and personalities. To help heal our then broken relationship, we began a spiritual journey that is still continuing.

On this giant boulder perch, we had an impromptu recommitment ceremony. We pledged our love and commitment to one another. Looking into Joyce's beautiful green eyes for longer than I usually do, I saw the most beautiful face I have ever seen, a face much too beautiful to be of this world. I was awestruck. It took my breath away, and at the same time I recognized that eternal face behind Joyce's face. It was supernatural and natural at the same time. It was extraordinary, yet so familiar. I knew and loved that

232   VISSELL

person that seemed to be someone else, yet was also more Joyce than the woman sitting across from me on the boulder. It was Joyce, and yet so much more than Joyce. It was Joyce in her ultimate perfection, which I have since referred to as her goddess self, or her higher self.

Interestingly, at the same time, I was revealing to Joyce my own divinity. There is no way to just witness the goddess in your beloved, without expressing your own higher self. Sure, it may be easier to see the goddess in your mate than to see and feel the god in you. But this is how it works. You can only see what you already are. If you want to see the goddess in her, but refuse to acknowledge the god in you, you are then blocking the process. Accept the god that you really are, and then the goddess in her will become visible and available to you.

In my own commitment to accept my god self, I have been blessed to witness the goddess in Joyce over the years. I consciously search for that holy essence of my wife. It has become a fundamental part of the way I love Joyce. Sometimes I see the goddess when we've been meditating or praying together, sometimes when we're making love, and sometimes at totally random times. Once it happened in a local restaurant. On our thirty-ninth anniversary on December 21, 2007, we went out to eat at a little restaurant in Santa Cruz. The mother of the owner, a woman our age from Sri Lanka, found out it was our anniversary. She shared that she had been married forty-three years and then bowed with hands together to salute us in a traditional Indian blessing.

When she told her son about us, he rushed over, gently took the menus from our hands, and told us he would bring us food to bless our holy union, and we should pay any amount we wanted. As we sat across from one another for the next two hours, this wonderful man intuited the foods and drinks that would best enhance our love. He brought Joyce a smoothie made from rose water and pomegranate juice, and me one made from pineapple and passion fruit. It was a sensuous feast. We felt truly honored and served like a queen and king. Even with the noise and distractions of a busy restaurant, Joyce and I entered a sacred bubble of love, impervious to all that was going on around us. And, through Joyce's eyes, I beheld the goddess in all her glory.

Joyce: It's the most wonderful feeling when Barry sees the Goddess in me. Usually it is something that happens both ways, like Barry described at the restaurant or sitting on the rock. He sees the Goddess in me and I see the God in him, and there is a beautiful flow back and forth. During these times, I both love being fully seen and also seeing him.

But it's even more special when I'm feeling anything but a Goddess and Barry still sees that in me. This past year has been a challenge for me physically. I tore a ligament in my ankle and had to wear an ugly black brace and, at the same time, developed plantar fasciitis, a painful condition in the heel of the same leg. After being treated for both conditions by my wonderful physical therapist, I should have

VISSELL

gone home and rested. Instead, I forced myself to do some errands even though my leg felt shaky and weak. I didn't notice the small curb until it was too late. I fell and broke my wrist and had to be in a cast. At this same time, a painful situation came up for someone I love very much and I was concerned and could not sleep well at night.

I felt like a wreck!!! I was limping through the house one day, barely able to walk on the injured foot, exhausted from yet another night of not sleeping well, when I saw Barry and asked him to help me tie my hiking boots, as I could no longer do that with my dominant hand in a cast. As he was tying my boots, Barry lovingly looked up into my face and just held my gaze.

"You're such a beautiful Goddess," he lovingly said.

"You're kidding me, right?" I responded in disbelief.

Very tenderly, he took my hand and said, "Your physical challenges, worry, and lack of sleep don't take away from your Goddess nature. You'll always be my Goddess and I love you very much."

I certainly did not feel like a Goddess. Yet, through Barry's love and vision of me as a Goddess, I opened to myself as being someone other than the pain-filled and emotionally upset person that I was feeling. I opened to the part of me that is more important than my body, and who has more faith and trust than I was feeling at the time.

I took our dogs for a walk in the woods. Rather than concentrating on my painful foot and ankle, the heaviness of my cast, and my worries, I concentrated on what Barry had said to me. With each step, the heaviness I had been feeling fell away and once again I started to feel like the person Barry saw in me. I returned home feeling ever so much better, just in time to catch Barry before he went off to play tennis with the guys. I looked at him and saw the God in him also, the loving man that I proudly married so many years ago.

Inner Practice: Communing with the Goddess

In the quiet of meditative reflection, after taking some deep quieting breaths, acknowledge you are more than your body, mind, feelings, and experiences. Give yourself a precious moment to accept your divinity, the being of light that you really are. Visualize and/or feel yourself as a being of light, with this light radiating from every part of you. Even physicists are discovering that the physical world is not so physical at all. Everything is made of energy.

If you skip this step, how can you expect to see the goddess in her? If you can accept, even a little bit, your own godhood, your own inherent light, the next part of the practice will flow naturally.

VISSELL

Now, picture the woman you love. Bring her face to face with you so you can clearly see her eyes. Even just doing this will often allow you to see her eternal being.

Next, imagine a light filling and surrounding her face. Even a glimpse of this light is enough to illumine her goddess self. Trust that this visualization is one of the highest ways to love yourself *and* her.

Outer Practice: Seeing the Goddess

Invite your partner to sit facing you. Make a date or set a time to do this practice. Let her know you want to do this practice. If she hasn't read this little chapter and practice, let her read it or read it to her.

Start with eyes closed. Acknowledge a higher power within you ... your eternal, spiritual, divine self.

When you're both ready, open your eyes and gaze into each other's eyes. This is not a staring contest! Practice "soft" eye contact by focusing on your breath and relaxing your abdomen. If you focus too much attention on what you see, and not enough on your breath and relaxing, you may abandon yourself in a way. The secret is to stay with your own god self, which will allow you to behold her goddess self.

You or your partner may not feel comfortable looking so deeply into one another's eyes. It takes practice, so don't be discouraged if one of you needs to stop before the other is ready. Also, don't be disappointed if her face seems to go through a series of changes, even faces that aren't familiar. This may be part of the process of the journey from the physical to the spiritual.

It can help to close your eyes for a while to regroup, then begin again. Each time you do this practice, you will become more and more comfortable with longer periods of eye contact. The goal is not to see how long you can look into one another's eyes. It's not a marathon! The goal is to catch a glimpse of the radiant, exquisitely beautiful eternal face of your beloved. Even a few seconds of seeing the light within her is enough to bring your relationship to a higher love.

May 18, 2004

Dearest Joyce,
Your love has completely transformed me.
Your devotion to God,
and God in me,
has made it easier for me to find and be with the
divine presence.
Your seeing me has made it easier for me to see
myself.
My birthday gift to you is my gift to you every
day of the year:
To protect you
so you can preserve your sensitivity and flower-
like essence,
To remind you of your beauty
so you never ever forget,
To listen to the symphony of your soul
so you know your voice and feelings are always
honored,
To bless your body and heart with my love and
adoration,
And to join with you,
uniting in the deepest place of oneness.
Your eternal lover and beloved,
Barry

The great poet, Rumi, says, "There are a thousand ways to kneel and kiss the ground." We sincerely hope you can also know there are a thousand ways (and more) to love a woman. May what we have written in this book inspire you to find even more ways.

About the Authors

The Vissells' books have been translated into five languages. They lecture and lead about 20 workshops per year internationally to audiences who welcome their warm, relaxed and yet profound wisdom. Joyce and Barry have written a monthly column for over 30 years, "New Dimensions of Relationship," which they email for free to their subscribers. These articles also appear in about 80 print publications internationally, and countless e-zines, web-sites (including their own), and blogs.

Ram Dass describes Joyce and Barry Vissell "as a couple who live the yoga of love and devotion." Marianne Williamson says, "I can't think of anything more important to the healing of our society than a connection between spirituality, relationship and parenthood. Bravo to the Vissells for helping us find the way."

Barry and Joyce are two people deeply in love since 1964, who have raised three children and "walk their talk." They are the authors of *The Shared Heart, Models of Love, Risk To Be Healed, The Heart's Wisdom, Meant To Be,* and *A Mother's Final Gift.* A story from *Meant To Be* was made into a Sunday Night NBC Movie, *"It Must Be Love,"* starring real-life couple, Ted Danson and Mary Steenburgen.

The Vissells, since 1983, are the founders and directors of the Shared Heart Foundation, a non-profit organization dedicated to changing the world one heart at a time (SharedHeart.org).

Joyce and Barry live at their retreat center and home near Santa Cruz, California, where they counsel individuals and couples, and lead retreats and trainings when they're not travelling.

Go to **SharedHeart.org** to sign up for their **free heartletter**, to read past articles on many aspects of personal growth and relationship, to see their event or workshop schedule, or to contact Barry or Joyce.

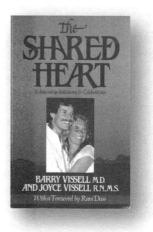

THE SHARED HEART

Relationship Initiations and Celebrations

ISBN 0-9612720-0-7, 186 pages, ©1984, Ramira Publishing, $9.95

The Shared Heart was one of the first books to bridge the chasm between following a spiritual path and having a deeply committed love relationship. As the book says, "Loving one other person teaches you how to love all people."

"The Shared Heart is full of beauty and compassion, richness and clarity. Barry and Joyce plough through the hard and soft spaces of the journey with great inner strength and deep respect for reflective inner tuning." —**Ram Dass**

"From the perspectives of romance, marriage, making love, parenting, careers, spiritual initiation, and loss of a loved one, this remarkable couple exhibits insight, acceptance and transcendence, at the same time offering specific tools for the transformational process of love."
—**Yoga Journal**

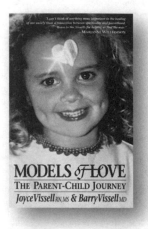

MODELS OF LOVE
The Parent-Child Journey
ISBN 0-9612720-1-5, 320 pages, ©1986,
Ramira Publishing, $12.95

Contributors include Jack Kornfield, Eileen Caddy, Leo Buscaglia, Jerry Jampolsky, Joan Hodgson, Jeannine Parvati Baker and others.

"Our children need not fall asleep to the beauty of their heavenly state for twenty, thirty, or more years, at which time breaking the habit of material thought is very difficult. We can help them begin the awakening process from the day they are conceived, so that the bridge of consciousness between the two worlds is continually strengthened."

"This is a book we whole-heartedly recommend to first-time parents, to grandparents, and to everyone in between."
—**Mothering Magazine**

*"*Models of Love *is more than a parenting book. It will bless your whole life!"* —**John Bradshaw**

"This book is full of miraculous incidents and sacred moments of loving connection that will bring tears to your eyes."
—**Whole Life Magazine**

"What society needs most is a connection between spirituality and parenthood. Bravo to the Vissells for helping us find the way"
—**Marianne Williamson.**

RISK TO BE HEALED
The Heart of Personal and Relationship Growth

ISBN 0-9612720-2-3, 192 pages, ©1989, Ramira Publishing, $9.95

Not infrequently, we receive an email or a letter with the words, "Your book has changed my life." Almost without exception, the writer is referring to *Risk to Be Healed*.

"In this book, Joyce & Barry offer the priceless gift of their own experience with relationship, commitment, vulnerability, and loss, along with the profound guide to healing that comes from the core of their being and blesses us with gentle wisdom."
—Gayle & Hugh Prather

The Vissells, in their uniquely captivating and personally revealing way, extend another written offering to the world. *Risk to be Healed* is filled with stories from their own continuing growth, as well as the healing risks individuals and couples have taken in their counseling sessions and workshops. The book begins with the profound experience of Anjel's death in utero and her subsequent birth into the lives of the authors. Subject matter includes: risk-taking in relationship, the way of intimacy, the power of right livelihood, understanding pain, healing relationships with those who have passed on, addictions, appreciation, vulnerability, and simplifying our lives.

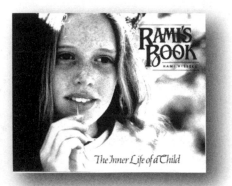

RAMI'S BOOK
The Inner Life of a Child
by Rami Vissell
ISBN 0-9612720-4-X, hardcover,
56 pages, full-color illustrated,
©1989, Ramira Publishing,
$13.95

"We have been taught for a long time that the entrance to God's presence is through the eyes of a child. Rami flings wide that delicious door of perception."
—**Rev. Stan Hampson, Past President, Association of Unity Churches**

"My hope is that all adults as well as children may benefit by the understanding and love that Rami shares in this delightful book."
—**Ken Keyes**

"Rami's book is a gift from an angel. The innocent beauty filling these pages brings me tears of joy. I wish children of all ages would read this book." —**Alan Cohen**

"Sensitively and endearingly written ... Rami's innocence and candidness is both moving and refreshing." —**Science of Thought Review, England**

"Of all the books I've reviewed, this one went right to my heart and made me cry quite wonderfully. Truly an angelic and marvelous work, and a gift to the child still within me. I put it on display with a sign: 'very, very highly recommended. 4 stars on the goose bump chart!'."
—**Richard Rodgers, manager, The Grateful Heart Bookstore.**

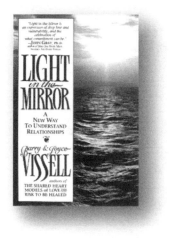

LIGHT IN THE MIRROR
A New Way to Understand Relationships
ISBN: 0-9612720-5-8, ©1995, Ramira Publishing, $13.95

"Light in the Mirror *is an expression of deep love and vulnerability, and the celebration of what commitment can be."* —**John Gray, PhD**, author of *Men Are From Mars, Women Are From Venus.*

"In Light in the Mirror, *Joyce and Barry Vissell share with deep tenderness and vulnerability the valleys and peaks of their relationship. They go on to share 'practical spirituality,' suggestions that will be most helpful to everyone finding their way home to the heart."* —**Gerald Jampolsky, MD** and **Diane Cirincione**, authors of *Love is the Answer* and *Change Your Mind, Change Your Life.*

"We have always benefited from the gentle wisdom of the Vissells. Light in the Mirror *is one of the rare voices for sanity in the field of relationships."* —**Gayle and Hugh Prather**, authors of *Notes to Myself* and *I Will Never Leave You.*

"If you had but one book to choose to renew your relationship, this should be the one." —**Small Press Magazine**

"Light in the Mirror is a must for anyone who yearns for better connection and more joy in their intimate relationships."
—**Napra Review**

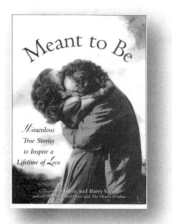

MEANT TO BE

Miraculous True Stories To Inspire A Lifetime Of Love
ISBN 1-57324-161-X, ©2000, Conari Press, $14.95

"The true miracle of these stories is that they open your heart to your own miracle, for the miracle of love is within you too, and your story can be as magical as these. That is the healing message on Meant to Be, that is its wonder."
– **Neale Donald Walsch**, author of *Conversations with God*

"Few books make me cry, but this one did, many times. The best collection of heart-full stories that I have ever read!"
– **Mary Jane Ryan**, author of *Random Acts of Kindness*

"The Vissells now bring us deeply moving (and some very entertaining) true accounts of Love's presence in the lives of other couples. Meant To Be says to us all, 'Relax. There are no chance encounters.'"
—**Hugh Prather**, author of *Notes to Myself*

"These wonderful stories remind us of the miracle that love is, and the magical ways it comes into our lives. Meant To Be *proves that, at the deepest levels, destiny is always at work in our lives.*"
—**Susannah Seton, author of Simple Pleasures**

A MOTHER'S FINAL GIFT

How One Woman's Courageous Dying Transformed Her Family

ISBN-13: 978-0-9612720-3-6, ©2011, Ramira Publishing, $14.95 US

"As we gave my mother her final gift on honoring her dying process, she gave us her final gift of opening a window into eternity and allowing us to have a peek."

A Mother's Final Gift is the story of one courageous woman – Louise Viola Swanson Wollenberg – and of her tremendous love of life and family, and her faith and resolve. But it is also the story of her equally courageous family who, in the process of rising to the occasion and carrying out Louise's long-held final wishes, not only overcame so many stigmas about the process of death but, at the same time, rediscovered what it means to celebrate life itself. This book not only touches the heart in a very powerful, poignant, and joyful way, but reading it was life-changing for me. In writing this book, Joyce and Barry Vissell, and their children, mentor us through an experience that many of us were afraid to even think about it. Louise looked at death as her greatest adventure. So should we all. The title of this book is indeed A Mother's Final Gift but, in truth, this story is an exceptional gift to every person who will read it.
– George Daugherty, Emmy Award-winning producer, director, and conductor